# Collected Works Volume Nine

## The Analysis

## Nigel Pearce

**chipmunkapublishing**
the mental health publisher

All rights reserved, no part of this publication may be reproduced by any means, electronic, mechanical photocopying, documentary, film or in any other format without prior written permission of the publisher.

>Published by
>Chipmunkapublishing
>United Kingdom

**http://www.chipmunkapublishing.com**

Copyright © Nigel Pearce 2023

The decline of bourgeois society means an intolerable exacerbation of social contradictions, which are transformed inevitably into personal contradictions, art suffers most from the decline and decay of bourgeois society. Art cannot save itself...But precisely in this path history has set a formidable snare for the artist.
- Leon Trotsky

Nigel Pearce

On Elise Cowen.

Why Elise? Why write about Elise Cowen? It is rhetorical; a Beat poet, they were the precursors to the counter-culture, obsessed with books, rejected her roots, depressive becoming psychotic, spent time in psychiatric hospital, and had ill physical health because of her drug use. She was different from many of her contemporaries and found it difficult to play the roles her generation attempted to impose on her; for this she would pay a high price, a premature death. Elise jumped through a closed seventh floor window to her death at the age of 29. Why did she crucify herself with hypodermic needles? I am 55 and may know, also having drug-related schizophrenia, a writer, but I have been 'clean' and 'dry' for over thirty years.

Since 2014 the conditions for a revaluation of her poetry existed with the publication of Elise Cowen's only complete notebook ['Fall 1959-Spring 1960'] Trigilio (2014) and of her life with the republication of Elise's friend's Joyce Johnston (2014) Come and Join the Dance in which Elise is Kay. This is in addition to her other primary source Johnston (2006) Minor Characters: a brief memoir of the Beat Generation and Skir (1970) Every Green Review, October 1970 both provide a wealth of material. The whole process of revealing this 'hidden history' of women 'Beat' writers could be traced to Neil Cassady's [the Muse of Allen Ginsberg and Jack Kerouac] partner Carolyn Cassady, who came out about the 'Beat' men in Cassady (1990) Off the Road: Twenty Years with

Cassady, Kerouac and Ginsberg. Her book was a sharp rebuke to the men of the Beat Generation. It was of course a pun on Jack Kerouac (2000) On the Road written in 1957 which was the cornerstone of male Beat fiction with Allen Ginsberg, he was intimately involved with Elise Cowen for a brief period, who's Howl (2014) was published, after an obscenity trial, in 1956 and provided the poetic foundation. I cast a shadow on the Beat's personal revolution as it did not produce a qualitative social transformation, a socialist revolution, only a quantitative shift in social values. Elise and I were writing as well. The Hit. 'Go man go.'   Elise encourages. As every junky knows there was a family dysfunction or three: Blessed Trinity. However, it is cast into Hades because Elise like I remembered that first hit of heroin. She said: What America needs is a lot of cheap heroin. Skir (1970) p10. Aged twelve, my mind was unlocked by L.S.D facilitating the comprehension of poetry: 'The force that through the green fuse drives the flower' (Thomas 1972, p. 8). Aged thirteen, I mixed with students like Elise, also an avid reader of Dylan Thomas (Skir 1970, p. 3).

We sought sanctuary in a company of souls who did not yell, new companions did not have the strut of oppression and welcomed all outsiders into the company of dreamers, and these people were not branded with the iron of hypocrisy. They caressed with potions, wondrous white powders which beckoned into worlds of meaning and caring. Initiating a world of compassion and the poetry of oblivion, they prepared our first fix. The

pristine white powder floated into a spoon, a
lighter ignites, a wait until the liquid began to
bubble with significance, cotton wool put in place
with the zeal of the mystic in the magic liquid, the
glass syringe sighed as the plunger is drawn up.
Hell would cease now, and the heavens danced to
caress the verse in the mind of the poets. Those
shackles floated away, the needle fitted snugly
onto the syringe, the singer of dreams smacked
our arms, the tubes became swollen, and the
spike pierced those purple veins, deliverance from
the world. As the plunger drew up a serpent of
blood danced into the cloudy liquid, a hit first time,
the plunger pushed this chemical dream out of the
syringe into my arm, her arm, we trembled
Arrr...warmth radiated up the arm rushing into the
catacombs which were minds now one... this heat
permeated the entirety of our body. We welcomed
the Kingdom; the stigmata on our arms were those
of a Beat beatitude. Elise wrote: Oh that I was a
Cunt of golden pleasure more pure than heroin or
heaven. Trigilio (2014) p.84. The Cellar.

The origins of 'New Woman' are in
Chernyshevsky (1863) What is to be Done
personified as Sonia Pavlovna. She fled her family
believing it to be dark and damp like a cellar. In a
similar manner Elise made what a revolutionary
move was for a young woman of nineteen from an
upper-class Jewish family with a definite Zionist
agenda. Joyce Johnston (2006) Minor Characters
articulated Elise's situation as she moved out of
the family 'cellar': Nineteen-year-old-girls did not
leave home except for dormitories or marriage. If

you lived free; you could not expect to live well.
Johnston (2006) p.63.

Existential psychiatry understood the roots of oppression and indeed the roots of insanity in the bourgeois family as David Cooper (1974) The Death of the Family wrote: We don't need Mother and Father anymore. All we need is mothering and fathering... Blood is thicker than water only in the sense of being the vitalizing stream of social stupidity. Cooper (1974) pp. 29-30.

Gilly rolled me a huge joint of rich green marijuana just as Allen Ginsberg had rolled one for Elise; we had both inhaled deeply and demonstratively. I had been 'underground', a 'missing minor' for some time. It was time for me to go down to the U.K version of Haight Ashbury in San Francisco, which was Notting Hill Gate in London, the hub of the counter-culture with the offices of Release, a drugs agency always willing to get you checked over by a 'cool' doctor. Hitched down the M1 from near Warwick University and got a 'lift', a lorry driver, a pleasant man. He asked when I last ate, then gave me his sandwich box and asked me my age, which was thirteen, I said 17. He dropped me at Newport Pagnell Services M1 brought me a meal and split. A brown Rover 2000 picked me up; the cat had his suit jacket hanging from a hook: 'Where are you going.' he asks. 'London, man.' I wore a red tee shirt, green jeans, desert boots and had a shoulder-bag made by my older sister as a present: 'I couldn't wait until you'd done your first trip' she said. 'I can drop you off wherever you want to go.' 'Err, possibly not man. Just where the motorway ends, thanks.' 'Have you been to any good orgies lately?' A shiver of fear shot through my frame: 'No man, they're not my scene.' We drove in silence to North London; I could tell he was no novice at this as we pulled into some run-down garages.

He stopped the car, unzipped his trousers, a little erect penis glared at me. 'Wank me off.' 'No, I don't want to.' 'I can get you as much heroin as you want.' I didn't believe him, grabbed the door handle and ran. He shouts: 'I killed someone last week for not doing it.' Years later I reflected that it was fortunate cars did not come equipped with central locking in the early 1970s. It was impossible to seek refuge in any way with the police, they were the 'enemy' as well when you're carrying drugs, a set of 'works'[8] and on the run. We had left these ostensibly 'nice people' for very genuine reasons, it just made sense: The Cowens were what my parents would call a nice family. Johnston (2006) p.54.

With a 'nice' apartment, 'nice possessions', nice and empty lives just like my parents and they were also similar in that: They raised their voices, though, a great deal. Mr. Cowen was given to threats and rages, Mrs Cowen to tears and recriminations. Johnston (2006) p.55.

My mother had been telling me she was going to 'commit suicide' since I was seven, since my sister became a hippie and run away from home. When I enquired further after about a year she said, 'I am letting off steam'. They put my sister in an 'approved school' to which I was taken as a child, it seemed friendlier than home. I was marked as if with a branding iron. Later she was put in a psychiatric hospital both of us apparently insane, but no one else knows the chill of a cellar and the fears there until you experience them. She didn't have the same interest in books; I think that is what saved me. Families can indeed seem like cellars from which we and many like us fled in fear. You go, break the chains or you would be processed by their huge machine Moloch as Ginsberg Howl (2014) warned against. Some of us were not ready to be butchered in their abattoir, but we knew that the cemetery beckoned, our names already carved upon the tombstones. Jehovah and other men. [I've tried] I've tried Been tried I'll try again Although my Beings weak There's nothing worth But God & you And God has gone to sleep. Trigilio (2014) p.49

There seemed to be three significant males prowling in Elise's life, all of them were Jewish like Elise and so they shared some concepts. Inevitably the God Jehovah as she was brought up in an upper middle class Jewish family. Although many Jewish émigrés embraced working class 'resistance ideologies' Anarchism in the case of Emma Goldman and Alexander Berkman which lead to an attempted assassination of the company director Mr. Frick in 1912. Allen Ginsberg's childhood was dominated by the American Communist Party and his mother's descent into insanity. I note, although Elise met Leo Skir at the Hechalutz Hazard camp in 1949, both rejected Zionism and Elise re-examined her

spiritual inheritance in her poetry and practice.
The second man as far as I can ascertain was Mr.
Cowen, another patriarch and the third was the
major Beat poet Allen Ginsberg. She was afraid of
the first two and fell in love with the third. Elise
attempted to reject the phallocentric nature of
post-war American culture in particular the God of
her childhood who cast a shadow of fear over her
life, the darkest of nights. She picks up a pen and
writes:
Jehovah, I don't believe a Word No, I don't believe
you care anymore Do you really want our fear
rather than our love? Trigilio (2014) p 42.
Ginsberg, (Miles 2010, p 172)

Mentioned, was trying to deny his homosexuality
at the time they met. Maybe that was a strand
within the thread of her infatuation for the Beat
poet. Ginsberg never seemed to say 'no' to very
much he thought would deepen his experience or
expand his consciousness [he also fought a long
battle with various strains of hepatitis]. She went
from being an outsider at Colombia University who
then had an affair with a philosophy professor to
being given the nickname 'Beat Alice' during 1953
because of her new involvement in Bohemian
circles.

I became 'another man' in Elise Cowen's life.
Influenced by the male Beat writers like William S.
Burroughs, Allen Ginsberg and Jack Kerouac from
an early age embracing the latter's belief in 'first
thought, first word' in my writing. The pen and
syringe were handed from their generation to the
generation of 1967 and then to my

contemporaries. Also, I shared their philosophical proclivities their strand of Existentialism: Nietzsche, Camus and Sartre. I embraced the Sisyphean moment, but Existentialism once realized can only be lived as practice, Praxis, because Camus (1976)

The Myth of Sisyphus argued that once Nietzsche had announced the 'death of God': There is but only one serious philosophical problem and this is suicide. Camus (1976) p.11. It is possible, I would argue, to perceive this very clearly in Elise, but also its ramifications for humanity in this post-modernist epoch. Click, my tape-recording cuts in: 'Revolutionary socialist current around Trotsky was in retreat, numerically tiny because of the betrayals of Stalinism and reformist Socialist Democracy the world became disorientated. Consumerism could never fulfil human needs and there were no other metanarratives.' Elise and her friends were in a storm without an eye, the rebels who had to make their own cause. Or so it might have appeared, but, Trotsky (1981)

Art and Literature understood there is never a linear line in literature; the dialectic exists to be answered by its antithesis. Literature cannot achieve that dialectical leap to a higher form of revolutionary literature without a movement lead by the 'universal class', the proletariat. Allen Ginsberg understood something of this: Holy the Fifth International. Ginsberg (2014) p.28. But his International to replace the Fourth International created by Trotsky could not attain its objectives by a dissident aestheticism, a new decadent movement which conjured up Baudelaire and 'art for art's sake' would not suffice. Elise would not have read Marx in depth, but her girlfriend Shelia, before the relationship with Ginsberg, had urged upon her return from Paris: Another French Revolution was necessary "blood must flow in the streets." Skir (1970) p.10. Elise merely commented about the necessity of cheap drugs, Leo Skir recalled. Her disorientation was increased, spinning like a whirling top out of control as she descended further into psychosis and addiction.

Elise's middle name Nadir meant 'nothing and nothingness' and she would have been aware of the pun on Jean-Paul Sartre Being and Nothingness (Kaufmann, 1969) as much of the 'Beat' scene was inspired by Existentialist philosophy. However, I was only to enter Elise's magical and dark world upon reading Knight (2006) and then I embarked on an odyssey which is achieving fruition in writing this piece of Life-Writing, I had almost lost my heart to this strange woman and certainly we were rather like twin meteors ablaze in a dark universe. Joyce Johnson, interviewed 3rd October 2002, said of Elise Cowen: The world treated her very badly because she was an odd girl. She didn't care about being pretty. She was, you know, very bright, and she was eccentric. Grace and Johnson (eds) (2004) p. 198. 'I'm waiting for the man.' I recollect living in squalid flat where The Velvet Underground and Nico L.P with the track 'I am waiting for the man', from their 1967 album, was played as if it were a Psalm. The song is about

'scoring' heroin and amphetamine, Elise must have waited for the man many times 'first thing you learn is you always have to wait' (Reed 2008, p. 3) lyrics continued. Elise would always be waiting for Allen Ginsberg and another futile wait that would be. Ginsberg's written choice of phrase, after her death, 'the intellectual madwoman' to describe Elise illustrates his lack of commitment to her. during their relationship Elise typed Ginsberg's long poem about his mother Kaddish. Joyce Johnston, Elise's best friend, encapsulated this in (2006) Minor Characters: A Beat Memoir: Elise was a moment in Allen's life. In Elise's, Allen was an eternity. Johnston (2006) p.78 Allen was, (Miles 2010, pp. 174-5) acting on the recommendations of his analyst who believed his homosexuality to be pathological and therefore encouraged him to have sexual relationships with women. Allen would soon fall in love with Peter Orlofsky, who became a lifelong partner.
Sigmund says... Elise was Skir (1970) informs us interested in Freud as were the other Beat writers. Burroughs famously 'analysing' Ginsberg, which was possibly traumatic for both. What did Freud say about the nature of the creative process in writers? A strong experience in the present awakens in the creative mind a memory of an earlier experience (usually belonging to his childhood) from which there now proceeds a wish which finds its fulfilment in the creative work?

The work itself exhibits elements of the recent provoking occasion as well as the old memory. Freud (1964) p.130 Freud compared the whole process to daydreaming. All of us and the Beats had concoctions allowing inner exploration. We all altered states of consciousness either to a lesser extent with hashish or marijuana or a greater extent with L.S.D or as Elise liked Peyote will recognise these. Certainly, in the creative person these can be far more intense. The hallucinogens produced, under favourable conditions an insight into the nature of oneself and the natural world or beyond, this was 'a good trip'. The 'bad trip' resembled something more like a descent into a Dantesque inferno. Lysergic acid diethylamide mimicked some of the experiences that are aspects of an untreated psychosis and as in the psychotic state the affected person can understand these as enlightening or intensely frightening. Often over time it is like a marriage of heaven and hell as with all mental illnesses and addiction or any substance misuse. For Elise these were a series of engagements with hell.

## The Last Trip.

A haze began to encircle us, with the desire to transcend this world and embrace an essence, something the 'elders' did not possess, ignited again within us. Two outcasts of the system, but within us burnt a love of the 'Idea'. We chose to live on the periphery, which is the body of Isis when she is pregnant with the 'Word'. A prophet of this tribe, Ginsberg, said he would give us 'Californian Sunshine' [L.S.D] for an 'ontological awakening.', but he hadn't intended that it should be taken intravenously. He cruised back later; the sacrament was laid silently in a sea of shadows, solitary in its wrapping of tin foil, awaiting an awakening, its benediction. Elise and I welcomed him, it was really his Mass, it is here she will celebrate the 'Word', the creative energy of the universe which comes from, the feminine, the Lunar Muse, Graves (1984) The White Goddess. Elise gently unwrapped the square of tin foil with long pale fingers and held it in her hands, Ginsberg raised it before his forehead and said in words like a priest as he holds the Eucharist: 'This is my body, take it and eat, you will be sustained by its vibrations and given a glimpse of infinity.' Elise and I genuflected before the Host, the Word: 'Have a good trip, never forget me.' Ginsberg waved goodbye. We were dizzy with anticipation as the sweet aroma of Isis scented our crash-pad. We quickly found the dream machine, prepared the 'gear' for a fix and located the mainline… wham without the fear of flying, we were left dancing. A spectre of William Blake appeared in the corner reciting: 'Hear the voice of the bard!

Who Present, Past & Future, sees; whose ears have heard The Holy Word that walked among the ancient trees.'

Tangerine lights merged into purple clocks which climbed the walls, their disembodied smiles swirled into seas of lemon, lime green flowers melt and kissed the skin, and then the mind dissolved into a pool of turquoise which wept back into the ceiling. They found me eight hours later curled into a ball, repeating a mantra: 'My name is Oedipus; my name is Oedipus, no more psychoanalysis'. Elise had already been admitted into Bellevue Hospital chanting: 'My name is Electra, my name is Electra, no my name is Emily, Emily Dickinson.' Emily Dickinson.

Elise had written three poems which referenced Emily Dickinson: Emily, Emily, white witch of Amherst and I took the skins of corpses:
[Emily] Emily, Come summer You'll take off your jewelled bees Which sting me I'll strip off my stinking jeans Hand in hand We're run outside Look straight at the sun A second time And get tan. Trigilio (2014) p.26. Elise originally concluded her poem with the line: And we'll hatch. She crossed out this line in her notebook (Trigilio 2014, p. 134) either an earlier rejection of motherhood as a choice of a woman Beat poet or possibly a reflection on an unwanted pregnancy with a drunken artist in California (Skir 1970, p. 8). This should have been a D&C but because of the long Christmas vacation the doctors performed a hysterectomy. The poem did suggest a feminist separatism, a sisterhood, which found a voice in the Feminist radicalization of the late 1960's and 1970's.

## Thanatos.

Elise like I didn't choose not to conform we just couldn't maybe we were too ill, the society we lived in was like a huge Praying mantis and in the end 'hip friends' disengaged. The Freudian opposite of the Pleasure Principle Eros, the death instinct Thanatos was very powerful in us both. Here a quote from Kay (Elise) as a young woman university drop-out [she did go back and Majored in Modern Poetry] in her friend Joyce Johnston's Come and Join the Dance, the first woman Beat novelist published in 1961:   'Well, I think I am going to be a failure," Kay said slowly. "I think that's already settled. And that's alright. But I want to be a magnificent one. A gigantic smoking ruin.' Johnston (2014) p 48. I was similar, but met exceptional therapists and nurses and with modern medicines can write and study.

Chipmunkapublishing and The Open University have become like paths through the desert which has led to a more fruitful life. The British philosophy David Hume thought people weren't a consistent 'Self', but rather a 'bundle of selves' like actors playing different parts on the stage of a theatre at various times.  Elise would write poignantly: Did I go mad…? [Extract] 'Did I go mad in my mother's womb? Waiting to get out … On my brain are welts from the moving that never moves On my brain are the welts from the endless stillness I don't want to intone "See how she suffers" "See how she suffers" (The sting of eyes reminds) That not really, or only what I mean- among other things I am not permitted to feel that much ... 'tick tock' 'But that the truth I guess of (Even were I to KNOW it) IS EVERYONE'S... Knight (2006) pp. 163-164.

Elise Cowen took her place with poets Sylvia Plath and Anne Sexton, women who had attacked the citadel of Patriarchal society, but consequently were cast into an abyss of the Great Patriarch. Self-destruction is a product of Patriarchal Capitalism and only mass proletarian revolution can create the conditions for the emancipation of poets, a golden dawn so sweetly scented with love's aroma. This maybe communism as envisaged by women writers like Alexandra Kollontai (1982) Love of Worker Bees in these circumstances Elise and I would not be stung by barbed wasps and we would live in a great hive together with the worker-poet's Queen Bee. We would write our poems with pens that have honey for ink and sup happily upon these sweet words. We would be humming with poetry, rather than buzzing with Benzedrine.

Maybe I was inculcated with the revolution as a child, but who knows, who remembers? I do. My poem about Elise: Elegy for Elise Cowen (1933-1962). Your smile is bright with magic, it draws in verse To glimpse the "straights", their vision is blurred And gazes inert, that form is carried in a hearse, But you who danced the naked poetics preferred The peace of wombs, the warmth, you "rush" induced seductress, Our wastes are frozen with promises, caught and chosen, This moth of candle and flame is burnt and wingless, At dawn you cupped it in a hand and have then written A dirge of deserts and biting sand which sings Into the syringe, enchantment of the finite "fix" Lies with accusations on pages scribed in blotted words, This sacred insanity is vibrating your soul, a matrix For jewels, the wind whispered opiate kiss, it is In here, where belief lies on the periphery, the poetry Ascends in grace with those of Auschwitz, You stumble across the graveyards and weep in symmetry. Pearce (2015) p 66.

**Bibliography.**

Camus, A (1976 [1955]) The Myth of Sisyphus, Harmondsworth: Penguin Modern Classics. Cassady, C (1990) Off the Road: Twenty Years with Cassady, Kerouac and Ginsberg. London: Flamingo. Chernyshevsky, N (1983 [1863]) What is to be Done, New York: Cornell University Press. Cooper, D (1974) The Death of the Family, Harmondsworth: Pelican books.

Freud, S (1964 [1959]) 'Creative Writing and Daydreaming.' The Standard Edition of the Complete Psychological Works of Sigmund Freud, Vol 9, London: The Hogarth Press.

Ginsberg, A (2014 [1956]) Howl and Other Poems, San Francisco: City Lights. Grace, Nancy. M and Johnson, Ronna. C (2004) Breaking the Rules of Cool: Interviewing and Reading Women Beat Writers, Mississippi: The University of Mississippi Press. Graves, R (1984 [1961]) The White Goddess, London: Faber & Faber. Kaufmann, W (1969) Existentialism from Dostoevsky to Sartre, Ohio: Meridian Books. Kerouac, J (2000 [1957]) On the Road, Harmondsworth: Penguin Modern Classics. Knight, B (2006) Women of the Beat Generation: the writers, artists and muses at the heart of a revolution, Berkley: Conart Press. Kollontai, A (1982 [1932]) Love of Worker Bees, London: Virago Johnston, J (2006) Minor Characters: A Beat Memoir, London: Methuen. Johnston, J (2014[1961]) Come and Join the Dance, New York: Open Road. Miles, B (2010) Allen Ginsberg Beat Poet, Great Britain: Virgin Books. Neale, D. (ed.) (2009) A Creative Writing Handbook, Milton Keynes/London: A & C Black in association with The Open University. Pearce, N

(2015) Icarus Rising: New and Selected Work, London: Chipmunkapublishing. Reed, L (2008) Pass Thro Fire: The Collected Lyrics, U.S.A: Da Capo Press. Sartre, J-P (1976[1943]) Being and Nothingness, London: Methuen & Co Ltd. Skir, L She was Beat with Allen Ginsberg: Elise Cowen: a brief memoir of the fifties, Every Green Review, October 1970. Thomas, D (1972) Collected Poems 1934-1952, London: Dent & Sons Ltd. On Method. Richard Holmes argues Life Writing has been profoundly transformed: People often suggest that the future of biography lies in a radical change of form- in the development of fractured or post-modern narrative models. But this has been going on for quite a time. Peter Ackroyd's original version of Dickens (1988) with its flamboyant insertions of fiction. Cline and Angier (2014) p 118. My interest was stimulated by Virginia Woolf's 'the lives of the obscure' (Lee (2009) p. 126). Lee continues: Biographies often speak for the alternative 'hidden lives', especially women's...- grew out of a feminist interest in 'hidden lives'...and of working-class history. Lee (2009) p. 127. Although sympathetic to these perspectives my methodology is derived from Marx: In the social production of their life, men enter into definite relations that are indispensable and independent of their will, relations of production which correspond to a definite stage of production. Solomon (1979) p. 29. There were three texts which were seminal in 'Life Writing' Dead Beat. Jean Rhys (1981) Smile Please which provided a material base for my episodic approach, Janet Frame (1984) Janet Frame: An Autobiography that blazed a path for the writing about mental health issues and thirdly, William S. Burroughs (2008) Junky which announced the historical moment that allowed people to write honestly about hard drugs. My method is derived from the practice of Life Writing as outlined in Haslam, H and Neale, D (2009) Life Writing and complexified in both Hermione Lee (2009) Biography: A Very Short Introduction and more recently in Cline, S and Angier, C (2014) Life Writing; A Writers & Readers Companion. Therefore, I am aware of the requirements of an opening paragraph elucidating one's motivation and the academic 'justification' for embarking on the manuscript. Also, I was made aware of the necessity of grounding the text in history, but also of the post-modernist breaking-up of simple narratives and a tendency towards the subverting of the genre. While Neale, D. (ed.) (2009) A Creative Writing Handbook taught me important lessons about Aristotelian poetics generally, the use of the dramatic method to enhance prose and the effective use of dialogue. Hence my idiolect is appropriate to the historical sense of 'place', the 'Beat Generation' and the 'counter-culture'. I 'cross-cut' in some sections and merge narratives. The usage of quasi- Roman Catholic metaphor is consistent with Jack Kerouac's usage of 'Beat' 'beatitude' which I extend in 'The Last Trip' to the Eucharistic: 'Take you all of this and eat' as metaphors for the consummation and consumption of the L.S.D. This surreal employment of language is entirely congruent with the 'altered state of consciousness' which it describes. Sergei Eisenstein's montage technique is used in, for instance, the descriptions of the family by Sonia Pavlovna, the biographical detail of the Cowen family and mine with Cooper's reflection on the redundancy of the family, which 'cuts' to a verbatim account of what happened when I hitchhiked down to London as a young adolescent. These linguistic, dramatic and cinematic devices were vital in allowing me to compose my manuscript, Dead Beat. The title is a play on words as in the premature death of a 'beat poet' and the now archaic American phrase 'dead-beat' i.e. exhausted. The authorial voice in my text is 'first-person plural.' In regard of the Aristotelian poetic Poetics (Aristotle 1996) I employ a 'dramatic arc' which articulates 'the whole': 'A whole is that which has a beginning, a middle and an end.' Aristotle (1996) p.13. There is a causal relationship between each section which I disrupt, writing in medias res. Neale (2009) comments on autobiography as a genre even when it is 'subverted': ... character is still it's most central and essential feature, just as in the more straightforward Robinson Crusoe. Neale (2009) p.7. Aristotle's concept was developed by Freytag (2004) and illustrated in Fig 3: Fig.3 I employ this structure and the conflicts which generate the 'action' are numerous e.g. familial and ideological. I recalled The Hours (Neale 2009, pp 350-54) and make use of Time and emblematic imagery, e.g. drug images. I use parallel stories; Elise Cowen's and mine with the same plot. Forster commented on the relationship between the story and the plot: The king died and then the queen died. The king died and then the queen died of grief. Forster (1955) p.86. The difference between the two, he argued, was the plot has a causal nature in an Aristotelian sense. A submerged and ordered sequence of action that creates a 'plot.' I would suggest that because of studying a Humanities Degree with Creative Writing at the Open University I have learnt to embrace 'the freedom of form'. I now have a far greater repertoire of technical devices and know better how to articulate my imagination. This is tantamount and consistent with asserting the module has allowed me to develop a 'creative voice'.   One invaluable lesson learnt was the discipline of Realism in a 'stage-drama'. As I was engaged with a concrete situation and compelled to physically move my characters upon a stage my abstraction had to be rooted in a material base. This was not a limiting experience, quite the opposite and with the use of Brecht's 'alienation effect' I was able to subvert Naturalism when I choose. Elizabeth Bishop correctly maintains of poetic 'forms': 'They seem to start the machinery.' (Neale 2009, p. 246).

 However, once learnt 'form' can be subverted as Elise Cowen and the Beat writers on the West Coast of America and the confessional' writers of the East Coast Establishment exhibited with consummate ability. The 'formal' and the 'experimental' can only complement. Is this not the paradox of modernism and post-modernism, the Metaphysical poets and Romanticism, and the debates about 'alienation effect' and Formalism in Socialist Realism which continue in Marxist circles? These apparent paradoxes are in fact dialectical in nature and each must therefore yes, contain a contradiction, but also a 'unity of

opposites' which must then create the dialectical leap to a higher stage, 'the negation of the negation' as delineated by Engels (1976) Dialectics of Nature: The law of the transformation of quantity into quality and vice versa;
The law of the interpenetration of opposites;
The law of the negation of the negation.
Engels (1976) p.62.


This is not a metaphysical Hegelian aesthetic, but rather one rooted in the production and reproduction of everyday life, the material creation of literature. Thus, the theoretical 'argument' that underpins my piece of Life Writing is that the Beat Generation as a social phenomenon could not produce the objective material or subjective conditions necessary for an Aristotelian eudemonia for outsider poets under capitalism. These poets like Elise and I would, it seems, only find creative fulfilment and emotional solace under the conditions of communism. I have not 'foregrounded' this as my tutor warned against an overly academic style. I have attempted to write balanced creative non-fiction as appropriate to Life Writing.

**Bibliography.**
Aristotle (1996) Poetics, London: Penguin Classics.
Burroughs, William. S (2008 [1953]) Junky, London: Penguin Classics.
Cline, S and Angier, C (2014) Life Writing; A Writers & Readers Companion. London: Bloomsbury. Engels, F (1976 [1883]) Dialectics of Nature, Moscow: Progress Publishers.
Forster. E. M (1955 [1927]) Aspects of the Novel, Harcourt, Brave & World: New York.
Frame, J (1984) Janet Frame: An Autobiography, London: The Women's Press.
Freytag (2004 [1863]) Technique of the Drama: An Exposition of Dramatic Composition and Art, Hawaii: University Press of the Pacific
Haslam, H and Neale, D (2009) Life Writing, London: Routledge in association with The Open University.
Lee, H (2009) Biography: A Very Short Introduction, Oxford: Oxford University Press.
Neale, D. (ed.) (2009) A Creative Writing Handbook, Milton Keynes/London: A & C Black in association with The Open University.
Rhys, J (1981) Smile Please: An Autobiography, Harmondsworth: Penguin Books

## Also On Elise Cowen.

On Elise Cowen (1933-1962):

Poetry on the Margins

"In the 1950's if you were male you could be a rebel, but if you were female your family had you locked-up. There were women, I knew them, their families put them in institutions, they were given electric shocks treatments".
- Scobie (1994).

During the 1950's in America a literary bohemianism developed which was similar to the decadence of late 19th century Paris, indeed the poetry of Charles Baudelaire and his essays on hashish helped form the psyche of the sub-culture which became known as 'Beat'.

'Hashish, like all other solitary delights, makes the individual useless to society, and also makes society unnecessary to the individual.'
- Baudelaire (1966) p39.

These writers and dreamers, rejected the mass consumerism of post war American society which was itself fuelled by arms spending (see Kidron (1968) for a Marxist analysis of how capitalism is temporary stabilized, economically, by arms spending) and embraced the 'new' in both art and life- style. They seperated themselves from mainstream or "straight" culture which they saw as bourgeois and corrupt with its "nice" families and "nice" people who were simply ideological replicas of the ruling class and its shallow culture. Indeed these "nice" people had bought the world to the brink of nuclear annihilation with a combination of U.S. imperialism and the consequences of the "degeneration" of the revolution in the Soviet Union.

The 'Beats' also rebelled against the stagnant literary forms and themes which had ossified western culture in the post-war period. William Burroughs used "cut-up technique" to create a surreal world in his novels e.g. 'Naked Lunch' and Allen Ginsberg transformed the world of poetry with his poem 'Howl' in 1956.They wrote about people who live on the existential edge, those who Jean-Paul Sartre said lived "authentically". Indeed Ginsberg's 'Howl' was inspired by Carl Solomon whom he had met in Bellevue mental hospital.

In the spring of 1953 Ginsberg and a young woman named Elise Cowen went out together on a "date". Elise had been born into a wealthy but unstable family:

'Mr Cowen was given to threats and rages; Mrs Cowen to recriminations and tears'.
- Johnson (1993) p (?).

As Elise had grown up she'd developed an aversion to "straight" society, locking herself in her room and reading Ezra Pound and Dylan Thomas. She began to neglect her appearance, but still went to university. Elise didn't succeed academically at college; but this was because she had an independent mind and spirit which wasn't subordinated to the dictates of her professors. Her state of mind began to deteriorate further at this time as she began to regularly use mind altering drugs, her poetry brilliantly sketches the demise into depression and later into psychosis:

Death ...

'Death I'm coming Wait for me
I know you're beat the subway station'

Here it is possible to be aware of Elise's knowledge of one of her favourite poets, Ezra Pound:

In a station at the Metro

'The apparition of these faces in a crowd; Petals on a wet, black bough'.

Ezra Pound (1975 p53).

Here both Pound and Cowen convey a sense of isolation and alienation from mass society.

...

Next Elise makes an (at the time) revolutionary comment on marriage:

Or wait till rot down with the
majestic orange she stuck on her finger
- Cowen (1996) p162.

Elise has expressed the absurdity of the 1950's American culture with a beautiful eloquence which is gained from having experienced the depths of depression and the 'highs' of amphetamine abuse. Her poetic technique breaks down the traditional form of earlier writers and the fragmentation of lines is suggestive of both a literary experimentation and a dislocated awareness, but most importantly it is an authentic consciousness in the face of death, which with the possibility of a nuclear war, the shadow which hung over the 'Beat' writers. Elise fell in love with Allen Ginsberg and thought they were "twin souls". In the same way as many people with mental illness do she perceived connections and associations which most people would not. Elise believed that because she and Ginsberg had both been patients, at different times, in Bellevue psychiatric hospital this was a 'sign' they should become lovers.

They and their friends were mostly poets centred round Colombia University, but they overlapped with some older writers, such as William Burroughs, with whom they would form the core of the Beat movement. They had a relationship, but Allen Ginsberg "came out" as being gay and moved in with Peter Orlovsky. He would always refer to Elise as "the intellectual madwoman". Her friend commented:

'Elise was a moment in Allen's life. In Elise's life Allen was an eternity'.
- Joyce Johnson (1983) p (?).

She began a love affair with a woman called Shelia, but this was a failure and other attempts to find the love she hadn't found in her family also proved to be fruitless. Elise was sometimes hospitalized, but she would seem more dispirited as a result. Her drug use increased at this time with the stimulants being used in conjunction with hallucinogenic drugs. The, almost, obsession of the 'Beat' poets with drugs and death can also be located in other revolutionary literary movements. An example of this is Romanticism [see Hayter (1968)]. Samuel Taylor Coleridge was a leading member of this movement, who wrote one of his most significant poems, 'Kubla Khan', under the influence of opium:

'In Xanadu did Kubla Khan'

A stately pleasure dome decree:

Where Alpha, the sacred river, ran Through caverns measureless to man Down to a sunless sea'.
- Coleridge (1996) p 229.

Coleridge's companion Thomas De Quincey claimed opium allowed him to: 'By signs in heaven-by changes on earth-by
pulses in secret rivers...and hieroglyphs written on the tablet of the brain...to gain the words'.
- De Quincey (1999) p 17.

This next poem gives us insight in Elise's state of mind as she declined into psychosis: Did I go mad...
'Did I go mad in my mother's womb

Waiting to get out
...

On my brain are welts from the moving that never moves On my brain are the welts from the endless stillness'
Here Elise describes the sometimes almost physical experience of mental illness, but also a sense of the descant into eternal void. Some within the 'Beat' movement were interested in a form of 'hip' Buddhism with the mystical states of nothingness being augmented by peyote.

'I don't want to intone "See how she suffers" "See how she suffers"

(The sting of eyes reminds) That not really, or only what. Elise is questioning the conventional domestic roles of women:

I mean-among other things I am not permitted to feel that much tick tock'

'But that the truth I guess of (Even were I to KNOW it) Is EVERYONE'S

And what is not this, is a rag flapping sometimes on the window in the wall across the shaft. Just more waiting, with bells on, And the Truth, is it only the FACT

of WAITING, the flash at the end of cosmic striptease?
I wants a little something for itself Unique, a single word, treasure act perfection
If only to give away Only to "He scatters his blood on the street."

Cowen now questions the purpose for her continuing existence:

'Love? Is this where, what, why Love, loving-all this time?'
- Cowen (1996) p 163.

By 1962 Elise had become very ill with hepatitis and psychosis and was admitted into Bellevue Hospital, she was discharged against doctor's advice into a private hospital. Whilst a patient there Elise's friend Leo Skir visited and later published parts of the conversation:

'She looked fine, better than I'd ever seen her,
neat, clean. But she was mad, quite mad. She felt
the City (New York City)
had machines trained on all her thoughts and also
that she could here them, the New York City
workers, foolish, bored, boring, mean-souled
people. She described to me in detail
the four people, two men, two women assigned to
her. 'Elise, I said, 'you're paranoid.'
'No,' she said, 'I'm not'.
- Skir (1970).

She was discharged into the 'care' of her parents,
they confined her and Elise jumped through a
closed window to her death. Cruelly her parents
destroyed Elise's poetry after her death; but

fortunately her friends had kept some copies. In
the study 'Minor Characters' Joyce Johnston
makes an incisive comment on Elise's life:

'She (Elise) could never put on a mask.'
- Johnson (1983) p (?).

Elise was never published in her life-time, but is
now regarded as an important Beat poet. Perhaps
William Burroughs encapsulates well the essence
of the 'Beat' writer:

'I'm a martyr to this fucking typewriter…but before
I'll ask help from the Commander I'll
write with blood and a hypodermic needle.'
- Burroughs (1999).p 153.

Like Icarus Elise and many others who have tried to solve their inner riddles flew close to the sun, the Truth, but it consumed them.

## Bibliography

Baudelaire, Charles (1999) [1966] Les Paradis artificiels in Writing on Drugs. London: Routledge.
Burroughs, William (1999) [1989] Interzone in Writing on Drugs. London: Routledge.
Coleridge, Samuel Taylor (1996) [1797] in Samuel Taylor Coleridge: Selected Poems. London: Penguin Books.
Cowen, Elise (1996) in Women of the Beat Generation. Berkeley: Conari Press.
De Quincey, Thomas (1999) [1822] Confessions of an English Opium-Eater in Writing on drugs. London: Routledge.
Hayter, Alethea (1968). Opium and the Romantic Imagination. London: Faber and Faber. Johnson, Joyce (1983) Minor Characters. London: Methuen.
Kidron, Mike (1968) Western Capitalism since the War. London.

Pound, Ezra (1975) Selected Poems 1908-1969.London: Faber and Faber.
Scobie (1974) from Stephen Scobie's account of the Naropa Institute tribute to Ginsberg, July 1974.
Skir, Leo (1970) Elise Cowen: A brief Memoir of the Fifties in Evergreen Review.

## On Allen Ginsberg, 'Howl' and Trotsky.

My argument is stated succinctly and argued to its conclusion. I contest that Allen Ginsberg's Howl was, as some critics argue a popular, 'an over-simplification' of the poetry regarded by the Canon as high-quality literature. Rather, Howl formed a new genre which mirrored in its innovation other seminal moments in literature connected to changes of the 'mode of production' and had similar ramifications. The 'primitive accumulation of capital of English capitalism' that Caudwell (1937) Illusion and Reality associated with William Shakespeare, the 'bourgeois' revolutions that permeate the ideas of Wordsworth (1802) Preface to Lyrical Ballads and the shocks of Darwinism, Freud and imperialist war which informed Modernist literature, particularly the avant-garde pertinently T.S.Eliot (1922) The Waste Land. What was the problem of the writer in late-capitalism as High Modernism entered its death throes? Trotsky (1981) Art and Politics encapsulate it: "The decline of bourgeois society means an intolerable exacerbation of social contradictions, which are transformed inevitably into personal contradictions, art suffers most from the decline and decay of bourgeois society. Art cannot save itself...But precisely in this path history has set a formidable snare for the artist." - Trotsky (1981). p 105. Ginsberg's reply is Howl, this is not the howl of the deranged madman outside of History, it resonates within the conversation of literature, King Lear (1603): "Howl, howl, howl! O, you are men of stones; Had I your tongues and eyes, I'd use them so That heaven's vault should crack." -

Shakespeare (1603) (5.3.2.58-64). Howl For Carl Solomon 1 I saw the best minds of my generation destroyed by madness, starving hysterical naked, dragging themselves through the negro streets at dawn looking for an angry fix, angelheaded hipster burning for the ancient heavenly connection to the starry dynamo in the machineery of night - Ginsberg (1956) p. 9 It is the howl of a post-WW 11 avant-garde that must inherently employ the poetic devices of literary tradition but in a different 'form'. A 'close reading' gives us several insights here. They are 'howls' of emotion, of intense emotion and resonate with William Wordsworth (1802) Preface to Lyrical Ballads: "Poetry is the spontaneous overflow of powerful feelings: it takes its origin from emotion recollected in tranquility." - William Wordsworth (1980) pp. 410-424. In Shakespeare (1603) we have a reference to the howling of a man driven to madness seeking justice from 'heaven's vaults'. Ginsberg also seeks refuge in chants to the 'Holy' in Footnote to Howl. The thematic howl of a literate madness, seeking divine justice, but not locating it in a corrupted 'world' runs counterintuitive against the whole Enlightenment project. Surely Reason and empiricist science will hear the poet's words. For Americans like Ginsberg the world could not be explained in these neat confines and as a poet who had read widely he certainly could not accept the text by text alone reductionism of the New Criticism after Hiroshima and McCarthyism, Auschwitz and Stalinism. But what differentiated Ginsberg from other 'Beat' writers in particular Kerouac was that he rejected Kerouac insistence on 'first thought, best thought'. Ginsberg was influenced by both Kerouac in terms of first impulse, but also poets like Eliot, indeed Howl' is an attempt at reproducing something of the literary magnitude of Eliot (1922) The Waste Land. I shall therefore argue against the perspective taken by advocates of Mass Culture Thesis such as the renegade ex-Trotskyist Dwight Macdonald, who argues in (1953) A Theory of Mass Culture and again (1962) Against the American Grain that the collective taste of the 'masses' was reflected in the degraded mass culture that they consumed and that, therefore, they had no 'interest' in 'High Culture'. Dwight Macdonald combined an ex-Trotskyist stance with cultural conservatism and elitism. Also, I argue against a rightist conservative position which is derived from Matthew Arnold (1869) Culture and Anarchy that has an inherent trepidation at the sound of the popular and its revolutionary proclivities. He maintained a 'secular religion' of "The best that has been thought and said in the world." - Arnold (1869) p 6. Was needed to prevent the erosion of civilization. It is no accident that Arnold began his opus magnum in 1867 after a period of popular and vigorous discontent over suffrage rights. Ginsberg's reply here is the 20th century equivalent to an articulate and insurrectionary mob assailing Arnold: "who dreamt and made incarnate gaps in Time & Space through images juxtaposed, and trapped the archangel of the soul between 2 visual images and joined the elemental verbs and set the noun and dash of consciousness together jumping with sensation of Pater Omnipotens Aeterna Deus to recreate the syntax and measure of poor human prose..." - Ginsberg 1956 p 20.

Arnold and his Leavisite descendants would be battered and lost for words, their Weltanschauung challenged. Also here we can perceive Ginsberg's specialist use of 'strophes' which he defines as 'a one speech breath thought' which was akin to the jazz improvisation of Miles Davis or Charlie Parker, the black man's 'beat'. 'Form' with a regard for socio-cultural factors would be engaged by the New Historicism of Raymond Williams with his 1958 Forward to Culture and Society: We live in an expanding culture, yet we spend much of our energy regretting the fact, rather than seeking to understand its nature and conditions. - Lodge (1972) p. 580. However, my position is not simply that Mass Culture Thesis and the New Criticism were erroneous, but they failed to understand the nuanced nature of 'proletarian literature' which as Trotsky illustrates is complexified: "Having broken up human relations into atoms, bourgeois society, had a great aim for itself. Personal emancipation was its name. In reality, all modern literature has been nothing but an enlargement of this theme." - Trotsky (1981) pp. 61-62. My position is that only the proletariat has the creative potential and socially universal nature which allowed Marx to say 'communism has solved the riddle of history' can transcend the limitations of the bourgeois intelligentsia when the social and economic conditions are ripe, that is, in a Socialist society because as Marx argued they are the 'universal class'. For the first time in history was there a social collectivity in whose interest it was to dismantle class society, because 'class' fetters on the workers of the world are their 'chains and it is in there interest 'collectively' to break those chains freeing the whole of society. Some Marxists misunderstood the nature of the relationship between the popular and the high cultures. Adorno and Horkheimer in Dialectic of Enlightenment saw an implied analogy between Marx's concept of his fetishized 'exchange value' as a commodity and 'use-value' a 'material object'. Then they extrapolated this analogy to the relationship between popular and high culture to the detriment of the popular. Walter Benjamin is better here, seeing the potential for mechanized reproduction to free the poet from the 'aura' from his or her primitivism and allow an engaged mass readership. Also, I will draw a parallel with Maxim Gorky, Lower Depths (see Raskin 2004 p.82) and Ginsberg Howl, thus Trotsky: "At the beginning, Gorky was imbued with the romantic individualism of the tramp. Nevertheless, he fed the early spring revolutionism of the proletariat on the eve of 1905, because he helped to awaken individuality in that class in which individuality, once awakened, seeks contact with other awakened individualities" - Trotsky (1981) p 58-59 For Trotsky the solution to the dichotomy of oversimplification and complexity in literature is resolved in the synthesis of revolution. Ginsberg, unlike Gorky would not be involved in a social revolution (as he may have wished) but a cultural revolution, a revolution of superstructure rather that of social base which left American capitalism weakened but intact. Louis Althusser (2006) Lenin on Philosophy and Other Essays commenting on the novels of Solzhenitsyn in (Althusser pp.153-153, 2006) makes the point of the difference between art and knowledge. Literature like Solzhenitsyn's, he argues, may have helped the reader 'feel' , 'perceive' the 'cult of personality' in the Soviet Union but doesn't provide the scientific knowledge to understand it. Althusser said art: "In the language of Spinoza it puts the conclusions before the premises." - Althusser (2010) p 153. Ginsberg achieves this by employing and developing poetic devices, Walt Whitman's 'long-line' which is a non-metrical line of poetry of length which usually employs enjambment, anaphora which is a 'figure of repetition' in which the same word is repeated as in Part 1 'Who' usually at the beginning successive 'lines, clauses or sentences' , cauda or the tail-rhyme stanza and a surrealist juxtaposition of images such as 'helium jukebox' (1956).Also Ginsberg aspired to create: 'Certain combinations of words and rhythms actually have "an electrochemical reaction on the body, which could catalyze specific states of consciousness." - Ginsberg (2001) p.31 Brain Jackson (2010) argues: 'the most compelling example of reading "Howl" -specially out loud – is the sene of time shifting from the prosaic to the mythical. Lines such as: "who walked all night with their shoes full of blood on the snowdeck docks waiting for a door in the East River to open to a room full of steamheat opium," - Ginsberg (1956) p. 15 He continues: 'the rhythmic and trouping artifice of Howl constitute...a suspension of time in which the natural laws occur'. - Jackson (2010) pp 312-313). Therefore I maintain that Ginsberg poetry contradicted the ideas of thinkers such as Mathew Arnold, T. S. Eliot, and William Empson's Seven Types of Ambiguity on the Right and renegade Trotskyists like Dwight MacDonald and neo-

Marxists Adorno and Horkheimer. I suggest that the neo-Marxism of Louis Althusser enhanced my general understanding of the positioning of the debates regarding the poetry of Ginsberg, particularly Howl and that in this context it is possible to comprehend him in a lineage of literati, Finally I argue that Ginsberg created not a simplified poetry for mass consumption and 'narcotization' of literary consciousness, but formed the matrix for a new genre of second wave of 20th century avant-garde writers who took and added to the High Modernism of 1910-39 and created a wedge into the monotonous conformity of 1950's poetry. Even poets like Sylvia Plath and Anne Sexton who were writing confessional verse which was challenging some conventions in terms of gender and 'content' i.e. mental illness Plath ([1963] 2004) Ariel and Sexton's (1960) 'To Bedlam and part way back' were not really contesting the terrain of bourgeois hegemony. Ginsberg did shift the aesthetics of the hegemonic superstructure cultural construct in favour of the 'progressive', he unlocks much in this poem, but he was unable to create a social revolution. I conclude that the task can only be brought to fruition by the self-emancipation of the proletariat as Leon Trotsky argues in Literature and Revolution: "Under Socialism, Literature and art will be tuned to a different key such as disinterested friendship, this will be the mighty ringing chords of Socialist poetry. However, does not an excess of solidarity, as the Nietzscheans fear, threaten to degenerate man into a sentimental, passive, herd animal? No, not at all. The powerful force of competition this, in bourgeois society, has the character of market competition, will not disappear in a Socialist society, but, to use the language of psychoanalysis, will be sublimated, Art then will become the most perfect ethos for progressive life-building of life in every field." - Leon Trotsky (1981). p 60 The Beats could not vanquish 'Moloch' (essentially, 'Capitalism') but they did undermine, disrupted what Lyotard calls it 'meta-narrative' creating the conditions for minority narratives. Nevertheless, only socialist transformation as understood in the aesthetic writings of Trotsky can create authentic liberation for all of humanity. We may read Ginsberg as a disappointed, reincarnated Maxim Gorky lapsing into a hope for Nirvana with a juxtaposition of the social and questioning 'Who' of Part 1, with the devastation of Moloch only relieved with the introspection of fifteen iambs in two sentences, one 'long-line' without punctuation except the repeated and insistent exclamation marks after each Holy! Footnote to Howl pp 27-8. Ginsberg did provide hope in a new 'beatification' of language within Historical Materialism's philosophy, a new Communist International to resurrect Trotsky's Fourth International... 'holy the Fifth International!' (ibid).

## Bibliography.

Adorno, T and Horkheimer, M. ([1944] 1979) Dialectic of Enlightenment, trans. by Cumming, London: New Left Books.

Althusser, L (2006) Lenin and Philosophy and other essays, Dahl: Aakar Books. Arnold, M ([1869] 1993) Culture and Anarchy and Other Writings, ed. by S.Collini, Cambridge: Cambridge University Press.

Caudwell, C ([1937]1977) Illusion and Reality, London: Lawrence & Wishart.

Eliot, T.S. ([1920] 1960) The Sacred Wood, London: Macmillan.

Empson, W ([1936] 1966) Seven types of Ambiguity, New York: New Directions.

Ginsberg, A ([1956] 2002) Howl and Other Poems, San Francisco: City Lights.

Ginsberg, A (2001) Spontaneous Mind: Selected Interviews 1958-1996. New York: HarperCollins.

Jackson, A, Modernist Looking: Surreal Impressions in the Poetry of Allen Ginsberg Texas Studies in Literature and Language, Vol. 52, No. 3, Fall 2010.

Lodge, J (1972) 20th Century Literary Criticism: A Reader, London: Longman. Lyotard, J.F. (1984) The Postmodern Condition: A Report on Knowledge, trans, by G. Bennington and B. Massumi, Manchester, Manchester University Press.

MacDonald, D (1953) A Theory of Mass Culture, Rosenberg, R. and White D.W (1957) (eds), Mass Culture: The popular arts in America, New York: MacMillan.

MacDonald, D (1962) Against the American Grain, New York: A Da Capo Paperback.
Plath, S (2004) Ariel: The Restored Edition, London: Faber and Faber.
Ruskin, J (2004) American Scream: Allen Ginsberg's Howl and the making of the Beat Generation, Berkley, University of California Press.
Sexton, A (1960) To Bedlam and part way back, Boston: Houghton Mifflin Company.
Shakespeare, W (1603) King Lear.
Pugh, T and Johnston, Margret R. (2014) Literary Studies A Practical Guide, New York: Routledge.
Trotsky, L (1981) On Literature and Art, New York Pathfinder Press.
Wordsworth W (1980) Selected Poetry and Prose of William Wordsworth, New York: Meriden Books.

On John Clare, labouring class poetics,
patronage, grammar, and madness:
A Gramscian analysis.
Some positional quotations.
An assertion made by Wordsworth about
Chatterton and Burns in the poem

Resolution and Independence:
We poets in our youth begin in gladness.
But thereof comes in the end despondency and
madness. (William Wordsworth, Resolution and
Independence, 1802)

Clare emerges for readers in this
society as a displaced, marginalized
poet whose reputation is gradually being
rehabilitated. . ... But it could be
that Clare—shy, feral, intensely gifted—will never
be redeemed from all the neglect and mutilation
he has suffered.

People expect originality... The truth is,
prisons and manicomi (mental institutes), are
packed with original types. Nevertheless, every
revolutionary has originality.

Marx has not written a catechism; he is not a
messiah who left a string of parables laden with
categorical imperatives of absolute, indisputable
norms outside the categories of time and space.
The only categorical imperative, the only norm, is:
'Workers of the world unite.'

...his way of viewing things is not a doctrine but a method. It does not provide ready-made dogmas, but criteria for further research.

The philosophy of praxis is consciousness full of contradictions, in which the philosopher himself, understood both individuality and as an entire group, not merely grasps the contradictions, but posits himself as an element of the contradictions and elevates this element to a principle of knowledge and therefore of action. .

Who has really attempted to follow up the explorations of Marx and Engels? I can only think of Gramsci.

Gramsci says of Dostoyevsky's work that it shows 'an awareness that the intellectuals have a mission towards the people'. Gramsci continues, 'The people may be "objectively" made up of the "humble" but they must be freed from this "humility", transformed and regenerated.

Clare's place in the tradition of English literature cannot be established by simple chronology or solely by reference to the leading writers of his age, though he was born just one year later than Shelley and lived until a year before Yeats was born. Since Clare continued to write from his adolescence until a few years before his death, he belongs chronologically to the age of Blake, Bloomfield, Scott, Crabbe, Coleridge, Byron, Shelley, Keats and Wordsworth.

It was taken for granted that a peasant poet was uneducated in a deliberate and specializing sense. Being uneducated implied a lack of the knowledge of formal grammar, yet at the same time it ensured a power to breakthrough established conventions, a freshness and a spontaneity of observation and feeling, the qualities that had supposedly been lost in the movement to a more artificial way of life and culture.

None of the supposed rights of man, therefore, go beyond the egoistic man … that is, an individual separated from the community, withdrawn into himself, wholly preoccupied with his private interest and acting in accordance with his private caprice. Man is far from being considered, in the rights of man, as a species-being; on the contrary, species-life itself – society – appears as a system which is external to the individual and a limitation of his original independence.

This thesis will contend that the employment of a Gramscian methodology enhances a reading of John Clare and that this advances scholarship of Clare. Following the logic of Historical Materialism, Antonio Gramsci's central concepts, such as Traditional and Organic intellectuals, Hegemony, and, therefore, counter-hegemonic intellectuals, cannot be understood as abstractions outside of the class struggle but should, instead, be applied to the 'lived experience' of concrete people and 'sensory activity.' Thus, I shall examine several areas in John Clare's concrete experience, considering Gramsci's key concepts. My first task is to position Gramscian theory and my argument in the intertextual narrative of Marxist literary criticism. Then, I shall examine the area of Clare and Gramscian theory applied to labouring class poetics, especially, the 'enclosure elegies' but also beyond this subgroup of Clare's poetry where relevant. That of two of his contemporaries, Ann Yearsley, and Robert Bloomfield. Here the relationship between Ann Yearsley and her patron, Hannah Moore, will be pertinent.

Therefore, the nature of patronage in labouring class poetics. Also, John Clare and his fraught relationship with John Taylor, notably regarding the question of grammar and dialect, is significant. I will explore Clare's 'madness' in Gramscian terms and, finally, explore the rupture between Marxist theory and the proletariat today, which is a pressing one, I argue. I will examine the prospects for a society where all can achieve their complete humanity, whereby the artificial and moribund division of labour between manual and mental labour will be abolished over time. Thus, this would allow the conditions for transcending John Clare's 'double alienation' from both his rustic roots and the literati. Finally, Clare's radical concern for ecology, as delineated in To a Fallen Elm is echoed in Charlotte Mew's The Trees are Down . Charlotte Mew's poem like some of Clare's asylum poems, is foreshadowing a certain demise. Both poems exhibit an extraordinary and profound discourse between the speaker and the natural world. As far as Mew's epigram is concerned from the Book of Revelation, it is of interest that Clare was involved with the Non-Conformist Christian group 'The Ranters' for a period in the late 1820s and early 1830s but not as early as 1820 as claimed by the Tibbles. This turn to a radical Christian sect was adequately informed by E.P. Thompson as 'the chiliasm of despair' in The Making of the English Working Class.

It is excellent to hear some of John Clare's poetry read aloud. However, compare John Keats Ode To a Nightingale' with John Clare's poem: 'A Nightingale's Nest' and see the aspirational bourgeois poet drawing on Classical sources. At the same time, Clare's poetry is literally grounded in the land to the extent that he gets scratched by a thorn bush. To deny the radicalism of Clare's verse in this respect would be ridiculous. Been reading Jonathan Bate's notes on the question of John Clare's texts and their evolutions which is probably the central scholarly debate in Clare's studies. Bate's research is certainly both extensive and impressive but vaguely impressionistic in my view in that it lacks a methodology. He fails to understand the site of Clare's texts, their normalization, and modification, beginning with his first editor and patrons, as arenas of class struggle. and, therefore, the contestation of cultural hegemony. The process which Clare delineated in poems like Helpston, to a Fallen Elm, The Lament of Swordy Well and, The Mores is one of counter-hegemonic resistance, which was incorporated by a 'passive revolution' in Britain, i.e. the granting of concessions by the ruling elite that was then comprehended by the masses as 'common sense.' Thus, I extend my use of Gramsci's method and insights.

## Chapter sequence.

## Introduction:

I make a new contribution to the scholarship on John Clare by placing it in a Gramscian context. This methodology cannot be abstracted from the narrative of Marxist literary criticism and philosophy or its concrete conditions. I will illustrate seven main areas.

Chapter One.

In search of a method.
I position my argument in the intertextual discourse of Marx & Engels, Plekhanov & Lenin, and Trotsky and Antonio Gramsci. Also, in the Anglophone tradition: Christopher Caudwell, E.P. Thompson, Raymond Williams, Perry Anderson, John Molyneux, and Alex Callinicos.

Chapter Two.

The pen and the sword.
I shall delineate John Clare's resistance to 'enclosure' and matters such as Byron's attack on the Labouring Class poets and understand these in Gramscian terms. Also, in this chapter, I shall explore the 'mosaic' (Gramsci) of folklore and its relationship to the role of the subaltern 'counter-hegemonic organic intellectual.' In the former case, as illustrated below in Alberto Mario Cirese (2022) Gramsci's Observations on folklore, Conceptions of the world, spontaneous

philosophy, and class instinct . He juxtaposes the folkloric tradition with the hegemonic:
folkloric versus official (active or passive) versus (active or passive) subaltern versus hegemonic simple versus cultured unorganic versus organic fragmentary versus unitary implicit versus explicit debased versus original.

Whereas the counter-hegemonic organic intellectual, in the last instance, contests hegemony with the terrain of the ethnopolitical elite.

Chapter Three.

'Money bags.'
The question of patronage was a thorny one affecting Yearsley and Moore. But was generalized to all labouring class poets. Kerri Andrews (2015) Ann Yearsley and Hannah More, Patronage and Poetry Routledge, London, will be seen as a valuable secondary source.


Chapter Four.

Grammar or Grammer.
...grammer in learning is like Tyranny in Government.
         - John Clare.

In this chapter, I will explore John Clare's counter-hegemonic 'voice' regarding his dialect and grammar and his attempts to defend it. The work of James C. McKusick, John Clare, and the

Tyranny of Grammar will be understood as a significant resource: https://www.proquest.com/docview/1297400775?parentSessionId=IEQIDHCnQfQcGqALrfFV1ZgCW%2Fbyij5SiexVc291JTw%3D&pq-origsite=primo&accountid=14697


Chapter Five.

Madness or double alienation.
Clare's opinion of Northampton County Lunatic Asylum was as follows:

> …there was never a more disgraceful deception than this place. The purgatorial hell & French Bastille of English liberty.

In this chapter, I will examine strands of Clare's 'madness' as an unstable counter-hegemony and also employ Classical Marxism's resources. Sara Lodge suggested that clinically, Clare might have experienced Cyclothymia which would not have justified hospitalization. I will investigate Clare's double alienation from his community and the literati, which will be understood in dialectical terms. Then it will be examined in the light of John Molyneux's (2021) The Dialectics of Art. Here Molyneux developed an innovative contribution to aesthetics with poetry being understood as non-alienated labour under capitalism when unified dialectically with 'Form and Content.' Marx argued that 'Milton wrote Paradise Lost in the manner that a silkworm produces silk. Of its nature.' Therefore,

Clare's 'madness' and double alienation may have been misunderstood. Bate (2003 p. 476) maintained that the reminiscences of a fellow patient, James Jerome provided valuable data which challenged the dominant narrative regarding Clare's illness, placing him in a more favourable light.


Chapter Six.

Western Marxism: results and prospects.

Following: Perry Anderson, (1976) Considerations on Western Marxism.
Alex Callinicos (2021), Routledge Handbook of Marxism and Post-Marxism.
John Molyneux (2022) Selected Works: Essays on Socialism and Revolution.
I also note the manner of Gramsci's assimilation into some areas of academia:
The conversion of an unrepentant Communist militant…into a harmless gadfly is undoubtedly among the most bizarre and distasteful episodes of recent intellectual fashion.
-P D Thomas, The Gramscian Moment, London, 2009, p 57fn.


I argue that since the failure of the October Revolution to spread to the advanced Western capitalist areas, there has been a growing gap between Marxist theory and the proletariat in the West.

Chapter Seven.

The conditions for John Clare's flourishing and the resolving of his double alienation under Socialism. It is difficult to predict the extent of self-government which the man of the future may reach or the heights to which he may carry his technique. Social construction and psycho-physical self-education will become two aspects of one and the same process. All the arts – literature, drama, painting, music and architecture will lend this process a beautiful form. More correctly, the shell in which the cultural construction and self-education of Communist man will be enclosed, will develop all the vital elements of contemporary art to the highest point. Man will become immeasurably stronger, wiser and subtler; his body will become more harmonized, his movements more rhythmic, his voice more musical. The forms of life will become dynamically dramatic. The average human type will rise to the heights of Aristotle, a Goethe or a Marx. And above this ridge, new peaks will rise.
 Trotsky (1924)
https://www.marxists.org/archive/trotsky/1924/lit_revo/ch08.htm
Furthermore, Clare's affinity with Nature and his opposition to enclosure provides insight into how, in a socialist society based on need and not accumulation, the impending climate catastrophe could be averted.

My inspiration is derived from E.P. Thompson:
I am seeking to resume the poor, the "obsolete" hand-loom weaver, the "utopian" artisan, and even the deluded follower of Joanna Southcott from the enormous condescension of prosperity.

The general methodology is drawn from Marx's Preface to A Contribution to the Critique of Political Economy (1859):
In the social production of their life, men enter into definite relations that are indispensable and independent of their will, relations of production which correspond to a definite stage of development of their material forces... The mode of production conditions the social, political, and intellectual life process in general.
- Karl Marx .

Therefore, I note Christopher Caudwell, in his early study of Marxian poetics, argued:
There is no neutral world of art, free from categories or determining causes. Art is a social activity…You must choose between class art which is unconscious of its causality and is therefore to that extent false and unfree, and proletarian art, which is becoming conscious of its causality and will consequently emerge as the truly free art of communism….

However, following the publication of Antonio Gramsci's theoretical material in English, Raymond Williams would suggest, and I agree, that:
        Gramsci's work…is one of the major turning points in Marxist cultural    history.

Thus, my argument furthers the scholarship on John Clare because it develops a Gramscian strand in that research and into the labouring class poetics more generally.

I shall illustrate that the term hegemony was not employed by Marx or Engels, although they did, of course, construct the argument of the artificial 'division of labour' between manual and mental labour as well as their conceptualization of 'ideology' in The German Ideology The German Ideology - Marxists which Gramsci would not have been able to access. The term came into use with Georgi Plekhanov in the 1880s and then with Lenin. This was the context in which Antonio Gramsci constructed his revolutionary and mould-breaking theory. Gramsci's ideas on intellectuals originated from Lenin (1901/1902). What is to be Done?

[…] all distinctions between workers and intellectuals... must be obliterated.
- V.I. Lenin.

See also Chris Harman:
The greatest modern theoretician of the philosophy of practice [i.e. Lenin] has in opposition to the various tendencies of economism...constructed the doctrine of hegemony as a complement to the theory of the state-as-force.

Although it is clear that for Gramsci, the state, rather than simply being 'a body of armed men' as Lenin had argued, was:

'the entire complex of practical and theoretical activities with which the ruling class not only justifies and maintains its dominance but manages to win the active consent of those over whom it rules.' i.e. hegemony.
Gramsci (1971) Selections from Prison Notebooks, p.244).

Although the Prison Notebooks presents two views of hegemony. Thus, the notion of hegemony can usefully be sketched using algebraic terms: Hegemony = consent + coercion = civil society + political society. Gramsci employs the formula: 'State = political society + civil society; in other words, hegemony is protected by the armour of coercion.' Antonio Gramsci delineated his theory of the organic intellectual in the context of his concept of hegemony, as explained here:
The general conclusion is thus clear: for a class to achieve hegemony, it has to create its own organic intellectuals who give that class consciousness of its role and educate it beyond the limited range of what Gramsci calls the 'economic-corporate level.'

As Gramsci poses the primary question about the nature of intellectuals, thus:
Are intellectuals an autonomous and independent social group, or does every social group have its own particular specialized category of intellectuals? The problem is a complex one, because of the variety of forms assumed to date by the real historical process of formation of the different categories of intellectuals.

Although it is important to recognize that Gramsci generally differentiated between the conditions pertaining to the 'East' (Tsarist Russia) about,' (Western Europe) in his epoch, his ideas here have, however, been positioned within two further Gramscian concepts. Firstly, a 'war of movement' and, secondly, a 'war of position.' The former term relates to Tsarist Russia, where the rule was by coercion rather than hegemony and was, thus, prone to a 'frontal assault,' i.e., the Bolshevik Revolution. The latter phrase refers to Western Europe, where a 'war of position' is necessary. Hence the revolutionary struggle became subsumed within a 'siege war' wherein the ideological and cultural struggles would be the necessary counter-hegemonic prerequisites for the coming revolution. Here we see Gramsci understanding the very concept of revolution in the 'West' as a continuum. It is important to emphasize that Gramsci's theorization of the West was not Reformist. He burrowed phrases from World War One and applied them to the class struggle. Later, I will examine the perspectives from (Anderson, 1976) and (Molyneux, 2022), explaining both the nature of Western Marxism and its rupture with proletarian activity. I would note Alex Callinicos's (2021), The Routledge Handbook on Marxism and Post Marxism argues for a new and fifth rendezvous between Marxist theory and the oppressed masses.

Hence, given the theoretical persuasiveness of Gramsci's ideas here. It becomes apparent these ideas are the shining path by which it is possible to illuminate women like Ann Yearsley and men like Robert Bloomfield and John Clare's Labouring Class Romantic poetry as they waged a counter-hegemonic 'war of position' against capitalism. Yearsley, Bloomfield, and Clare were not in what Marx, referring to Shelley, had called 'the revolutionary vanguard.' They had no 'vanguard' organization nor the advantages that poets like Shelley, from the aristocracy, and Keats, the rising bourgeoisie, had bestowed upon them. Also, the proletariat had not, yet, coalesced into the instrument of social transformation. So, these poets were 'counter-hegemonic' in the sense that a 'war of position' was their only option if they were not to be bludgeoned into submission and obscurity in their epoch.

Therefore, I shall argue that John Clare was an 'organic intellectual' who, in the 'enclosure elegies,' his relations with patrons and publishers and in the 'asylum poems' was a counter-hegemonic voice. Here is an example of an enclosure elegy, although, as Sara Guyer (2015, p. 80) notes, 'the Enclosure Act of 1809 was only implemented in 1820, the year in which Clare's first volume of poetry was published.' However, it is central to my account of the first strand within Clare's 'counter-hegemonic account as follows:

Enclosure came, and trampled on the grave /
Of labour's rights/ left the poor a slave. [...]
A board sticks up to notice 'no road here.'
And on the tree with ivy overhung
The hated sign by vulgar taste is hung
As though the very birds should learn to know
When they go there, they must no further go…

The phrase 'enclosure elegies' emanated from Johannes Clare's (1987) John Clare and the Bounds of Circumstance. The nature of his counter-hegemonic struggle can be understood herein in his trespassing poetry. We can see John Clare in The Village Minstrel, (1823) stanza 102, articulating three years after the Enclosure Act was enforced, a nascent proletarian class consciousness:

The toil-worn thresher, in his little cot
Whose roof did shield his birth, and still remains
His dwelling place, how rough soe'er his lot,
His toil though hard, and small the wage he gains
How would he turn and look, and linger there,
And wish e'en now his cot and poverty to share.
That many a child most piningly maintains;
Send him to distant scenes and better fare,
How would his bosom yearn with parting-pains
Although this was reminiscent of Wordsworth's (1798), The Ruined Cottage. John Taylor, Clare's publisher, as noted in John Clare, The Trespasser (John Goodridge and R.K.R Thornton, 2016, p.59), wrote in the manuscript: 'This is radical Slang.' Therefore, we can observe the class differentiation and the power relationship between the publisher and the published.

Here I show Byron's assault on Labouring class poets:
Lo! Burns and, nay, a greater far,
Gifford was born beneath an adverse star,
Forsook the labours of a servile state,
Stemmed the rude storm, and triumphed over Pate:

Then why no more? if Phoebes smiled on you,
Bloomfield! why not on brother Nathan too?
Him too the Mania, not the Muse, has seized;
Not inspiration, but a mind diseased:
And now no Boor can seek his last abode,
No common be enclosed without an ode.
And in contrast, John Clare wrote about his fellow Labouring Class poet, Robert Bloomfield. The change in both language and tone is stark:
   Our English Theocritus, Bloomfield.

Thus, I show the class struggle was intense on occasion, for as Marx and Engels (1848) Communist Manifesto argued:
The history of all hitherto existing society is the history of class struggles. Freeman and slave, patrician and plebeian, lord and serf, guild-master, and journeyman, in a word, oppressor and oppressed, stood in constant opposition to one another, carried on an uninterrupted, now hidden, now open fight, a fight that each time ended, either in a revolutionary reconstitution of society at large or in the common ruin of the contending classes.

   Clare's conflicts with various patrons were reminiscent of Ann Yearsley and Hannah Moore:
The parallels between Yearsley and Bloomfield…as well as Clare… suggest Yearsley was not particularly belligerent or ungracious. Indeed, she might usefully be seen as the most public face of what appear to have been relatively commonplace tensions and disagreements which ran through patronage relationships towards the end of the eighteenth century.

I also delineate his efforts and contestation with the publisher, John Taylor, over attempts to preserve his dialect and original grammar. An example of attempts by Clare to reject the 'hegemony of Official Standard English' (Tom Paulin (1992) John Clare in Babylon pp.47-55) is in a letter to Taylor dated 21st February 1822 in which he wrote: [misspelling grammar] 'Grammer in learning is like Tyranny in government' (1951) [eds] Tibble J.W & Anne, The Letters of John Clare, p.133. In this context, I note: James C. McKusick, John Clare and the Tyranny of Grammar:

It is the locality of Clare's dialect that irritates his critics; the Scottish dialect, having a distinct national character, poses no threat to England's national identity. But if the "rustics" of Northamptonshire, Lancashire, and Somerset are allowed to publish their local dialects, the cultural and linguistic hegemony of London will be exposed and eventually destabilized. These are some of the latent political issues at stake in Taylor's editing of Clare's poetry.

I agree with John Goodridge (2013) John Clare and Community regarding the dialectics of Labouring Class poetics between classes but also between isolation and collectivism both between classes and within those classes. I show that Clare's, sense of isolation from his class is illustrated in his prose (note his spelling of 'cumb for 'come'):

As I did not like to let anybody see me reading on the road of a working day I cumb …into Burghley Park and nestled at the wall side.

John Clare's madness can be perceived as a counter-hegemonic instability. It consisted of two major currents. Firstly, his 'delusion' that his childhood sweetheart Mary Joyce was a 'second wife.' In order to marry her, he absconded from the High Beech private lunatic asylum on 20th July 1841. He might have met a young Tennyson during his stay (Bate, 2005, pp.431-432)

But after leaving walked eighty miles, sometimes living on grass, eating nothing for a forty-eight-hour period, only to find she had died in 1838 in a house fire. In Clare's epoch and circumstances, he could not have known she was dead when he absconded from High Beech asylum, although he thought he had glimpsed her twelve months earlier. I postulate that Byron would not have been detained in an asylum for believing that he had more than one wife. It was a question of class and behaving in a fashion not appropriate to a 'peasant poet.' He was behaving in a counter-hegemonic manner which was an element that led to his detention in Northamptonshire County Lunatic Asylum, where he would stay until his death twenty-three years later. He wrote between eight hundred and one hundred and seventy-six asylum poems while incarcerated privately in both asylums. Those surviving are contained in Poems of John Clare's madness, ed. with an introduction by Geoffrey Grigson (London, 1949) and Poems of the Later Period (1964) eds Eric Robinson &

Geoffrey Summerfield. His second period of hospitalization was paid for by Lord Fitzwilliam at eleven shillings a week in Northamptonshire Lunatic Asylum.

The official reason for his detention was recorded as:
   A farmer addicted to Poetical prossing. The question of multiple personalities arose as Clare was recorded as saying:
      I am John Clare now. I was Byron and Shakespeare   formerly. At different times you know I am different people
   – that is the same person with different names
Clare would describe the latter hospital as follows:
      …there was never a more disgraceful deception than this place.
         The purgatorial hell & French Bastille of English liberty.



Therefore, I argue that to utilize Gramsci:
   All men are intellectuals; one could therefore say: but not  all men have in society the function of intellectuals.
-   Antonio Gramsci

   Retrospectively, Perry Anderson encapsulated the two distinct traits of Western Marxism, which of course, Gramsci was a leading theoretical practitioner of as well as an activist:

The circle of traits defining Western Marxism as a distinct tradition can now be summarised. Born of the failure of the proletarian revolution in the advanced zones of European capitalism after the First World War, it developed an ever-increasing scission between socialist theory and working-class practice.

Therefore, I have attempted to construct a Gramscian analysis of John Clare within the narrative of Labouring Class Poetry. As well as an explanation of what John Molyneux (Molyneux, 2022, p.45) has designated as 'the rift between socialism and the working class.' Although it is worth assimilating the data regarding the size of the working class, which is now far larger than when Marx and Engels in the Communist Manifesto argued (Helen Macfarlane's translation, 1851), 'Proletarians of the world unite.' Hence, it is possible to argue that there is the potential for a fifth revolutionary rendezvous between Marxism and the proletariat, as Alex Callinicos (2021) suggested:
The evident conflict between the logic of capital and the urgent necessity of reconstructing our economies to begin to heal the metabolic rift from which spring the catastrophes now cascading on us offers probably the most promising terrain on which Marxist ideas, in no doubt some unanticipated form, can become a material force once again.

Both my study of John Clare's poetry and of the theoretical apparatus employed, as well as the problems identified within Marxist theory, such as its reception by the proletariat in Western conditions, further the current scholarship, and this, could create a rich theoretical current for other researchers.

Nevertheless, I also argue that The Law of the Tendency of the Rate of Profit to Fall, as discovered by Marx, will create the objective conditions for socialism, but as Trotsky (1938) The Transitional Program noted that it is often subjective factors like, for instance, 'the immaturity of the proletariat.' (Trotsky,1938) that influence the harvesting of ripe objective economic conditions for the creation of international socialism. Nevertheless, a combination of economic crises and dialectical clashes of oppressed and oppressor means the circumstance for socialism will reoccur and either succeed or, quoting Marx: 'lead to the common ruin of the contending classes.'

In conclusion, I argue that someone like John Clare, although a counter-hegemonic organic intellectual, would only resolve his inner contradictions in a socialist society, as argued by Trotsky (1924). Here he suggested that every person would become 'an Aristotle, a Goethe, a Marx '. It is only then that we can become fully human, I suggest. Nevertheless, I return to the Prison Notebooks of Antonio Gramsci:
In reality, one can only scientifically foresee the struggle but not the concrete moments of the struggle'

Finally, I note that Gramsci complexified the Leninist theory of the State and the relationships of power: For Gramsci, the state, rather than

simply being 'a body of armed men' as Lenin had argued, was:
 'The entire complex of practical and theoretical activities with which the ruling class not only justifies and maintains its dominance but manages to win the active consent of those over whom it rules.' i.e. hegemony.
 ((1971) Selections from Prison Notebooks, p.244).

Therefore, these are the limitations of the Marxist theory and of possible human knowledge. This noteworthy poem, written in Northamptonshire County Lunatic Asylum, illustrates the devastation that was inflicted upon Clare for being a counter-hegemonic organic intellectual:

I Am!
I am—yet what I am none cares or knows;
My friends forsake me like a memory lost:
I am the self-consumer of my woes—
They rise and vanish in oblivious host,
Like shadows in love's frenzied stifled throes
And yet I am, and live—like vapours tossed

Into the nothingness of scorn and noise,
Into the living sea of waking dreams,
Where there is neither sense of life or joys,
But the vast shipwreck of my life's esteems;
Even the dearest that I loved the best
Are strange—nay, rather, stranger than the rest.
[…].

Swimming against the stream is always a challenge especially if, firstly you are not part of a revolutionary wave in what Gramsci called 'an organic crisis' where a new counter-hegemonic 'social block' contests power on the 'ethno political' level and secondary if you, like Clare, are torn by 'contradictory consciousness' as Gramsci explained thus:

two theoretical consciousnesses (or one contradictory consciousness): one which is implicit in his activity and which in reality unites him with all his fellow-workers in the practical transformation of the real world; and one, superficially explicit or verbal, which he has inherited from the past and uncritically absorbed. But this verbal conception is not without consequences. It holds together a specific social group, it influences moral conduct and the direction of will, with varying efficacity but often powerful enough to produce a situation in which the contradictory state of consciousness does not permit of any action, any decision or any choice, and produces a condition of moral and political passivity.

## Appendix 1.

The research questions and concepts that supply the underpinnings of this doctoral proposal are, firstly, why should I endeavor to construct a reading of John Clare? This was answered in the secondary literature by E. P. Thompson (1968, p.13) The Making of the English Working Class: 'recover from the enormous condescension of prosperity.' Secondly, what is my method and why? I place my response in the intertextual discourse of Marxist Literary criticism. An innovative development within this tradition was mentioned by Raymond Williams (1977), Marxism and Literature: 'Gramsci....is one of the major turning points in Marxist cultural theory.' Thirdly, why does Gramsci's explanatory framework assist in supplying a satisfactory model for enhanced reading of John Clare's contribution to English Literature? This is because he developed the ground-breaking idea of Hegemony and associated it with the innovative concept of the 'counter-hegemonic organic intellectual.' Thus, I question the reading of Joanne Clare's (1987) John Clare and the Bounds of Circumstance, in which she argues that Clare, although aware of his class identity, was not a revolutionary poet. Was Clare a revolutionary poet? Possibly not in the manner that Marx described Shelley as 'being in the revolutionary vanguard.' He did not have the social advantages that Shelley possessed and, rather to utilize Gramsci's terminology, fought a 'war of position' rather than an overt one, a war of movement' as pursued by the aristocracy and nascent bourgeoisie such as John Keats.

Another research question is whether Clare was mentally ill to the point of hospitalization. Sara Lodge argues that he may have experienced Cyclothymia which would not have justified detention in asylums. This is congruent with Clare's letters. So, I argue there is a synthesis between John Clare's life and the contemporary 'lived experience ' of numerous psychiatric patients in modernity.

However, my research questions spread further than the individualization of one member of a social collectivity, labouring class poets of the Romantic Period. My thesis will ask and answer questions such as those of women labouring class poets like Ann Yearsley. Their writing and life. In particular, the question of patronage was relevant to all Labouring Class poets of this period and which, I note, Dickens, in his one reference to John Clare, was scornful. Regarding women poets. What was their attitude to social and gender questions in their epoch? What was the reception of women's Labouring Class Romantic poetry, and did it differ from that of men like John Clare and Robert Bloomfield?

Returning specifically to John Clare, I am interested in his relationship with his editor, John Taylor, especially regarding questions of editing and grammar. This, I shall contend, was an arena for class contestation.

My concluding section of research investigations covers two fields, closely related, to my methodology. Firstly, the nature and failure of Western Marxism to make a connection with the proletariat and, what would be the nature of social formulation which would favour poets, indeed humanity. The question of ecology is a pertinent one.

## Appendix 2.

An excellent quote on the 'philosophy of praxis':

... at the level of theory Philosophy of Praxis
cannot be confounded with or reduced
to any other philosophy. Its originality lies not only
in its transcending of previous philosophies but
also and above all in that it opens up a
completely new road, renewing from head to toe
the whole way of conceiving philosophy itself.
 - Antonio Gramsci.

The philosophy of an epoch... is, therefore,
nothing other than the 'history' of that epoch itself,
nothing other than the mass of variations
that the leading group has succeeded in imposing
on preceding reality.
History and philosophy are in this sense
indivisible. They form a 'bloc'.
 - Antonio Gramsci.


On Passive Revolution:

The process, for Gramsci, whereby the bourgeois
gradually transforms itself to retain power. In Italy,
after the Red Years of 1919/1921, Fascism came
to power and stabilised the hegemonic group but
left in place capitalism's contradictions. Also,
Gramsci understood how Fordism or Americanism
in the period of the Recession managed to
increase the 'rate of exploitation' (productivity) by
introducing its regimented factory system and
essentially bribed the proletariat with a few extra

commodities but left unresolved the questions of History, i.e. the Social Revolution. More specifically, Gramsci drew this concept from the comparison between the active Jacobian revolution in France and its passive counterpart in Italy during the latter part of the 19th century in Italy which did not disturb the relations of power but created a gradual metamorphosis of superficial change which did not call into the question the hegemony of society's elites.

## Appendix 3.

*Autumn*

The thistledown's flying, though the winds are all still,
On the green grass now lying, now mounting the hill,
The spring from the fountain now boils like a pot;
Through stones past the counting it bubbles red-hot.

The ground parched and cracked is like overbaked bread,
The greensward all wracked is, bents dried up and dead.
The fallow fields glitter like water indeed,
And gossamers twitter, flung from weed unto weed.

Hill-tops like hot iron glitter bright in the sun,
And the rivers we're eying burn to gold as they run;
Burning hot is the ground, liquid gold is the air;
Whoever looks round sees Eternity there.

This belongs to the group of poems written while Clare was confined in the Northampton County Asylum from 1842 until his death in 1864.

Here we can comprehend Clare's transforming 'weeds' i.e., commoners into an integral aspect of their environment. Here Clare overcomes the alienation of man, the subject, and nature, the object with a holistic, indeed, organic

understanding. In Gramscian terms, Clare has written beyond the fragmentary and inorganic 'mosaic' of 'folk culture' to provide an innovative reading by a 'counter-hegemonic organic intellectual.' The authentic 'gold' of Nature is seen as elemental in contrast to the gold of the bourgeois literati and that of those in power over him in Northampton
County Asylum.


*A Vision.*

I lost the love of heaven above,
I spurned the lust of earth below,
I felt the sweets of fancied love
And hell itself my only foe.

I lost earth's joys but felt the glow
Of heaven's flame abound in me
Till loveliness and I did grow
The bard of immortality.

I loved but woman fell away
I hid me from her faded fame,
I snatched the sun's eternal ray
And wrote till earth was but a name

In every language upon earth,
On every shore, o'er every sea,
I give my name immortal birth
And kept my spirit with the free.

In another asylum poem, Clare attempts to create an ordered poetic form for his 'contradictory consciousness' (Gramsci). It is of note that the first three stanzas use anaphora in the repeated 'I's. He is a poet alone, alienated in Feuerbachian terms from 'heaven above' but locates his 'species-being' (Marx) in writing. There is a certain ambiguity about women which can also be found in his two Byronic poems  Don Juan and Childe Harold's Pilgrimage which were both composed in High Beech private asylum. It is written in iambic tetrameter rhyming abab bcbX  cdcd  ecec. The anaphoric 'I suggest a possible narcissism but, I would contend, the repeated emphasis on the 'self' suggests a contended 'self' and a 'counter-hegemonic instability.' So, therefore, A Gramscian reading illuminates the reading in both its concept of 'contradictory consciousness' having elements of primitive culture and those of a labouring class poet concluding on line 16: 'And kept my spirit with the free.'

Nigel Pearce

*The Lament of Swordy Well.*

[...]

Yet worried with a greedy pack
 They rend and delve and tear
The very grass from off my back
  I've scarce a rag to wear....


There was a time my bit of ground
  Made freeman o...e slave...[...]

The gypsies camp was not afraid
  I made his dwelling free
Til vile enclosure came and made
  A parish slave of me...[...]


Clare, in this poem of protest and pain, employs his intimate knowledge of Swordy Well to not merely rebuke the act of enclosing the land and, thus, carving up both the land itself and the tradition of the 'open field system' in which three fields would be rotated by those who worked them. Also, leaving a piece of 'common land' on which the local agricultural workers could hold festivals, herd a cow, or suchlike. This, the enclosing of land so amended by Clare was felt deeply. It was the destruction of the life he and those before him had known. That is not to construct a rustic idyll because living off the land was hard. However, the whole sense of community was swept away by this privatization of the common land and commodification of the open field system. This is precisely why Clare personified Swordy Well. It was an integral part of him and of the bucolic community. Clare here transcends Wordsworth and Keats in that, although empathetic, they looked in from the outside rather than Clare; it was an act of mutilation of both his body and mind. In this sense, it can be argued that in defending the past, he was looking to a future society based on the village commune. This was not the conception that Lenin or Gramsci argued for but a late letter from Marx does suggest the village commune in Russia could provide a model for a socialist society. Therefore, it could be argued by extension that here Clare was performing the role of an intellectual embedded in his developing class, an 'organic intellectual' to employ Gramsci's phrase.



Further poetry by Clare on enclosure:

When reformations formidable foes
 Wi civil wars on natures peace combind
& desolation struck her deadly blows
As curst improvment gan his fields inclose
-John Clare, The Village Minstrel, II 1049-52.

Enclosure like a Buonaparte let not a thing remain
It levelled every bush and tree and levelled every hill and hung the moles for traitors (ll. 67-69)
-       John Clare, Remembrances.

John Lucas = Swing Riots moles etc.

   If [...] I try to break down those bounds, it is not because

  I think that having done so I can prove Clare to be in any    unambiguous sense a committed radical poet. The point is rather that an attentive reading of his poems and the    circumstances of his life will suggest that his political views cannot be stabilised, for the very good reason that

  he himself was subject to (and of) so many contradictory  forces as to put stability or consistency out of reach

-       John Lucas, 'Clare's Politics', Haughton, pp. 148-77 (p. 148).


John Lucas commenting on Johanne Clare (1987) John Clare: Beyond the Bonds of Circumstance. While Johanne Clare (1987) suggests that the full significance of Clare's contribution to English literature is found not in his social criticism but in his refusal to dissociate himself from his past or to become assimilated into the mainstream of English culture at the expense of his class-identity. She argues that a clear set of aesthetic principles informs his finest work and provides the first thematic and structural classification of his poetry. Focussing on the major vocational poems and selected passages from the prose, she shows how Clare formulated the creative ideas and rhetorical techniques that allowed him to give unified expression to both his social and literary concerns. Clare's deep involvement with nature and rural England was the basis for his poetry and enabled him to articulate beliefs that opposed his time's inhumane values.

## *THE HOLLOW TREE*

How oft a summer shower hath started me
To seek for shelter in a hollow tree
Old huge ash-dotterel wasted to a shell
Whose vigorous head still grew and flourished well
Where ten might sit upon the battered floor
And still look round discovering room for more
And he who chose a hermit life to share
Might have a door and make a cabin there
They seemed so like a house that our desires
Would call them so and make our gipsey fires
And eat field dinners of the juicey peas
Till we were wet and drabbled to the knees
But in our old tree-house rain as it might
Not one drop fell although it rained till night

Bate, Jonathan. Song of the Earth. Pan Macmillan. Kindle Edition, location 2644.

## Appendix 4. On Stuart Hall.

Has been reminded of Stuart Hall's important work on popular culture as a site of contestation. Hall relied on several influences, including the culturalism of British Marxist thinkers like Raymond Williams and E.P. Thompson, the import of Althusser, possibly most importantly Gramsci's thinking on hegemony and organic intellectuals, but also the 'multi-accentuality' of Volosinov in Marxism and the Philosophy of Language. I did not agree with every dot and comma when I studied for my first degree at the Open University in Political and Social Science when it was under the influence of Hall. Still, there is no doubt he brewed up something intellectually potent. In the last instance, much of his thinking can be understood as a product of the British working class in a 'downturn'(Tony Cliff) and the lack of sophisticated Trotskyist analysis. Nevertheless, he is remembered as an important Left thinker.

The 'organic intellectual' must work on two fronts at one and the same time. On the one hand, he has to be at the forefront of intellectual, theoretical work...But the second aspect is just as crucial: that the organic intellectual cannot absolve himself or herself of transmitting those ideas, that knowledge...to those who do not belong, professionally, in the intellectual class?
-Stuart Hall (1992) Cultural studies and its theoretical legacies, p.281.

Stuart Hall on Popular Culture in the context of Gramsci's 'hegemony.'

Because popular culture is 'relational', not static in its orientation to the 'ruling bloc.' It is the most important arena for class contestation. However, there is, therefore, no binary opposition in manners of understanding popular culture:

a) The obvious definition of popular culture understands the 'masses' as 'cultural dopes' unable to discern the quality of cultural artefacts thrown at them. Storey (1983) shows that 80% of new album releases fail even with advertising.

b) The mechanistic Left position proposes that there is an 'authentic proletarian culture' which is 'sighed' with 'resistance that will overthrow the bourgeois culture. This was not Trotsky's position, who believed the proletariat must learn from the bourgeois culture before a proletarian one becomes possible. Bogdanov and the 'Productionists took a different view after October 1917, arguing for a 'proletarian culture.'

c) For Hall the site of popular culture does not have a fixed inherent nature:

popular forms become enhanced (and degraded) in cultural value, go up and down the cultural escalator.

- Stuart Hall (1981) Notes on deconstructing the popular. p.234.


Also, I agree with Peter D. Thomas (2009), The Gramscian Moment, London, Haymarket, that Perry Anderson eluded the significance of Gramsci's discovery in April 1932 of the concept of

the 'integral state' in the West. A beautiful application of dialectics.
Here is Gramsci:

"a point of no return: the dialectical 'identity-distinction between civil and political society."
This was a unique contribution from Antonio Gramsci.

## Appendix 5. On ecology and Johnathan Bate's Song to the Earth.

There are some fairly uninformed readings of Marx in both of these books, i.e. Ecocriticism: New Critical Idiom. Bate is more sophisticated but does not seem particularly acquainted with the early Marx (1844) Philosophical and Economic Manuscripts, which is unfortunate and has no Trotskyist critique of the USSR. His intellectual gymnastics as far as Romantic poetry are somewhat beguiling but his reliance on Heidegger is unfortunate. Although the three questions the later Heidegger asked are interesting, 1) What are poets for? (Wozu Dichter?) although he first asked this question on the death of Rainer Maria Rilke, which dates to 1926! But later, in 1953, he added What is the essence of technology? 'He added,' What does it mean to dwell on Earth? I am just uncomfortable with Bate's use of a Heideggerian methodology.

For my liking, Bate uses the word 'cosmic' a little too frequently in his reading of John Clare. Here is an opening gambit before he moves on to Martin Heidegger:
'I have found a language for my response to this poem in a book published in 1958 by the French philosopher and historian of science Gaston Bachelard. Entitled The Poetics of Space, its subject is what Bachelard calls the ontology of the poetic. He is interested in the way that through the brilliance of a poetic image, 'the distant past resounds with echoes, and it is hard to know at what depth these echoes will reverberate and die

away'. For Bachelard, the poetic image has its distinctive being in this quality of reverberation, which is an overcoming of time. But we can only understand the image's being by ourselves experiencing the reverberation. Bachelard thus calls for a mode of reading that is a listening rather than an interrogation. He considers himself a felicitous rather than a severe reader.'
Bate, Jonathan. Song of the Earth. Pan Macmillan. Kindle Edition.

## Appendix 6. On the Pastoral.


Theocritus and Virgil's poetry are a contested arena now. The Pastoral is not entirely as it was when John Clare argued:
'Bloomfield, England's Theocritus.'
Of course, Clare's referencing another Labouring-class poet is significant for my purposes. Equally, Milton: Paradise Lost is an Epic that those writing in the Anglophone tradition will always be in its shadow. Harold Bloom reckoned John Clare was 'a Wordsworthian shadow.' However, I have never been entirely convinced of Bloom's fundamental concepts.

John Middleton Murry proclaimed, 'The intensity with which Clare adored the country which he knew is without a parallel in English literature; of him, it seems hardly a metaphor to say he was an actual part of the countryside.'
This is something of a theme in that while Wordsworth was looking in at Nature, Clare was part of it. My comparison of Keats To a Nightingale and Clare A Nightingale's Nest is where the speaker scratches themself on thistles while observing the nest in the latter.

Has been looking at Schiller's essay On Naive and Sentimental poetry. German Romanticism was important for Anglophone poets.

Therefore, many critics reading of John Clare, in the light of Schiller's differentiation between Naive (those describing directly) and Sentimental poetry (self-reflective writing), place Clare in the former category. I am not totally convinced of this dichotomy.

*The Anti-Pastoral.*

Stephen Duck (1736) The Thresher's Labour was the first example of this genre in English literature. He spoke from a labouring class perspective yet was answered for his sexism by another labouring class poet, Mary Collier (1739) The Woman's Labour: An Epistle To Mr Stephen Duck.
 Donna Landry argues that labouring-class women poets such as Mary Collier, a laundress, and Ann Yearsley, a milkwoman, transformed the anti-pastoral with their alternative detail of women's actual pastoral work, not just in producing 'a counter-discourse to this class-conscious, largely masculine tradition', but in helping 'produce transformations within the georgic mode' (Landry 1990: 23),

Gifford, Terry. Pastoral (The New Critical Idiom) (p. 124). Taylor and Francis. Kindle Edition.

Duck had written that after a day's haymaking 'Next Day the Cocks appear in equal Rows'. Mary Collier replied that it was the women who made them suddenly appear next day. After a brief mid-day break, soon we must get up again, And nimbly turn our Hay upon the Plain; Nay, rake and prow it in, the Case is clear; Or how should Cocks in equal Rows appear? (Collier 1989: 17)

Gifford, Terry. Pastoral (The New Critical Idiom) (p. 123). Taylor and Francis. Kindle Edition.

*Gramsci: basic concepts:*

Civil Society.

Gramsci uses this term to designate 'the ensemble of organisms commonly called "private" ' (p . 306) , that is to say the sum of social activities and institutions which are not directly part of the government, the judiciary or the repressive bodies (police, armed forces). Trade unions and other voluntary associations , as well as church organisations and political parties, when the latter do not form part of the government , are all part of civil society . Civil society is the sphere in which a domin ant social group organizes consent and hegemony, as opposed to political society where it rules by coercion and direct domination . It is also a sphere where the dominated social groups may organize their opposition and where an alternative hegemony may be constructed .

Gramsci, Antonio ; Forgacs, David. The Antonio Gramsci Reader: Selected Writings 1916-1935 (pp. 637-638). New York University Press. Kindle Edition.

*Common sense.*

Everyone, for Gramsci , has a number of 'conceptions of the world', which often tend to b e in contradiction with one another and therefore form an incoherent whole. Many of these conceptions are imposed and absorbed passively from outside, or from the past, and are accepted and lived uncritically. In this case, they constitute what Gramsci calls 'common sense' (or, in another context, 'folklore') . Many elements in popular common sense contribute to people's subordination by making situations of inequality and oppression appear to them as natural and unchangeable. Nevertheless, common sense must not be thought of as 'false consciousness ' or as ideology in a merely negative sense. It is contradictory - it contains elements of truth as well as elements of misrepresentation - and it is upon these contradictions that leverage may be obtain ed in a 'struggle of political "hegemonies" '. For Gramsci it was important that Marxism should not present itself as an abstract philosophy but should enter people's common sense , giving them a more critical understanding of their own situation. See in particular Section XI and 'philosophy of praxis' in this glossary).

Gramsci, Antonio ; Forgacs, David. The Antonio Gramsci Reader: Selected Writings 1916-1935 (pp. 638-639). New York University Press. Kindle Edition.

*Economic-corporate.*

This term is always used , overtly or implicitly, in opposition to 'hegemonic'. 'Economic-corporate' interest means the collective interest of a particular economic category: for instance, merchants , or engineering workers . For a social group to become hegemonic, it must move not only from economic-corporate consciousness to class consciousness; it must also go further since class Becoming hegemonic may well mean sacrificing economic class interest in order to build 'expansive ' alliances. See on this the description of successive 'moments' in the formation of collective political consciousness in 'Some Aspects of the Southern Question ' (p. 174) and 'Analysis of Situations: Relations of Force ' (pp. 205-6).

Gramsci, Antonio ; Forgacs, David. The Antonio Gramsci Reader: Selected Writings 1916-1935 (p. 639- 640). New York University Press. Kindle Edition.

*Economism:*

Economism means for Gramsci the theoretical separation of the economic dimension from a social and political ensemble: more specifically, the reduction of this ensemble to its economic causes . Economism is epitomised in his view not only by the 'mechanical historical materialism' of the Second International (1889-1914) but also by revolutionary syndicalism and bourgeois liberalism (or laissez-faire) , which in this respect he assimilates to one another. The former privileges the revolutionary transformation of economic production at the ' expense of the winning of political power and the transformation of the state . The latter sees the economy as a self-regulating sphere of individual enterprise to be separated from the interventions of the state. Yet, in reality, the state is necessary to sustain a capitalist economy and bourgeois society, and historically it increasingly intervenes in them. In contrast with economism, Gramsci develops the concepts of hegemony and historical bloc (q.v.).

Gramsci, Antonio ; Forgacs, David. The Antonio Gramsci Reader: Selected Writings 1916-1935 (p. 640). New York University Press. Kindle Edition.

*Hegemony.*

This term appears to have entered Gramsci's usage from the political vocabulary of Russian Social Democracy and the Third International (for a fuller discussion, see Anderson 1976-7: 15-20 and Buci-Glucksmann 19 80 : 174-85). In this context the word meant leadership of a class alliance : in a first instance (referred to the 1905 revolution) proletarian leadership of the bourgeois democratic revolution ; subsequently (after 19 17) proletarian leadership of an alliance with the peasantry and other exploited groups . This leadership is based on the economically central role of the leading class but it is secured politically by that class's making economic concessions and sacrifices to its allies. In Gramsci's 1926 essay 'Some Aspects of the Southern Question', he argues (p . 173 in this edition) that the proletariat can only become hegemonic, a ruling class, if it ca n overcome its economic self-interest and win the support of the poor peasantry and southern intellectuals . This notion, which develops out of Soviet debates in 1923-26 , recurs in the prison notebooks (see for instance VI.IO, 'Analysis of

Situations: Relations of Force'). It becomes closely associated with two other concepts: 'Jacobinism' and the 'nation al-popular' and opposed to two others: 'economism' and 'economic-corporatism' (q.v.). Hegemony in this sense is necessarily rooted in an economically dominant, or potentially dominant, mode of production and in one of the 'fundamental' social classes (bourgeoisie or proletariat), but it is defined precisely by an expansion beyond economic class interest into the sphere of political direction through a system of class alliances. In the prison notebooks this meaning of 'hegemony' remains but the term is extended in two ways. Firstly, it is applied not just to situations of proletarian leadership but also to the rule of other classes at other periods of history. Secondly, it is qualitatively modified : hegemony comes to mean 'cultural, moral and ideological leadership over allied and subordinate groups. Hegemony in this sense (which Gramsci develops through the mediation of Croce's concept of the 'ethico-political') is identified with the formation of a new ideological 'terrain', with political, cultural and moral leadership and with consent (VI.5). Hegemony is thus linked by Gramsci in a chain of associations and oppositions to 'civil society' as against 'political society', to consent as against coerci on, to 'direction' as against 'domination'. (X.l). These binaries draw on the coercion-consent opposition in Machiavelli and some other political thinkers. Gramsci 's concept of hegemony als() appears to have been influence d by historical linguistics in its accounts of the influence or 'prestige' exerted by one form of a language over another.

Hegemony in Gramsci is sometimes interpreted as a relation purely of cultural or ideological influence or as a sphere of pure consent; it is also sometimes assimilated to the notion of 'dominant ideology' (see for instance Hunt 1986:215 and Boggs 1976) . Yet these interpretations seem to be mistaken. Gramsci stresses that 'though hegemony is ethico-political, it must also be economic, must necessarily be based on the decisive function exercised by the leading group in the decisive nucleus of economic activity.' (pp . 211-2) In cases such as that of the French parliamentary regime 'the "normal" exercise of hegemony ... is characterized by the combination of fo rce and consent variously balancing one another' (VIII .2, my emphasis) . He also insists that hegemony is dynamic (a 'continuous process of formation and superseding of unstable equilibria and that 'the fact of hegemony presupposes that account be taken of the interests and the tendencies of th e groups over which hegemony is to be exercised'. (p. 21 1) In other words it presupposes an active and practical involvement of the hegemonized groups , quite unlike the static , totalizing and passive subordination implied by the dominant ideology concept . It also seems in correct to maintain that, since Gramsci applies the concept of hegemony not only to proletarian revolutionary leadership (as in the Russian tradition ) but also to bourgeois rule, this means that he sees the bourgeois and proletarian rule as being structurally assimilable to one another or as containing a sort of interchangeable core .. Gramsci is, in fact, careful to distinguish different forms of hegemony according to the different historical situations and the class actors involved. Typical forms of bourgeois hegemony are 'passive revolution' and 'transformism ' (q.v.) or that of the parliamentary regime. By contrast, Gramsci defines proletarian hegemony indirectly when he writes of the philosophy of praxis (q.v. ): 'It is not an instrument of government of dominant groups in order to grasp the consent of and exercise hegemony over subaltern classes; it is the expression of these subaltern classes who want to educate themselves in the art of government ... ' (VI . 7)

Gramsci, Antonio ; Forgacs, David. The Antonio Gramsci Reader: Selected Writings 1916-1935 (pp. 641-644). New York University Press. Kindle Edition.

*Intellectuals*

Gramsci defines intellectuals in the prison notebooks as those people who give a fundamental social group 'homogeneity and awareness of its own function'. Intel lectu als are educators , organizers , leaders . 'Organic' intellectuals are those who emerge from out of th e group itself: for instance a worker who becomes a political activist . 'Traditional' intellectuals are those who have remained from earlier social formations and who may attach themselves to one or the other fundamental class: for instance, priests, who may have either a revolutionary or a conservative function depending on their class identifications. In the political party organic and traditional intellectuals come together. In Italian the term 'intellectual work' (lavoro intellettuale) also has the sense simply of 'mental work ' or 'work by brain'. In both cases 'intellectual' defines a function as much as it defines th e concrete individual who fulfils this function . envisage a situation in which , as Gramsci is thus able to part of the revolutionary transformation of society , the intellectual function is massively expand ed - in other words more and more pe ople share th e tasks of mental activity , of organizing , deliberating and leading, both politically and within the sphere of economic production. For Gramsci this would also be a process of democratisation and would inhibit the formation of bureaucracies, which arise precisely where decision-making is mon o polarized by a specialized elite of intellectuals. Intellectual and moral reformation Gramsci adapts this term , via George s Sorel , from Ernest Renan (one of whose books was entitled La Reforme intellectuelle et morale) and applies it , by analogy with the Reformation and the French Revolution , to a Protestant wholesale transformation of conceptions of the world and norms of conduct brought about by the philosophy of praxis (q.v.).

Gramsci, Antonio ; Forgacs, David. The Antonio Gramsci Reader: Selected Writings 1916-1935 (pp. 645-646). New York University Press. Kindle Edition.

## Jacobinism

In Gramsci's early writings the term 'Jacobinism' has negative connotations of sectarian, mystical, abstract, elitist (see for instance III.2; also SPW I, pp. 32, 170, 309). In the prison notebooks, however, it is 'revalued' and acquires the positive meaning of leadership of a national-popular alliance in which the peasant masses are organically bonded to the leading class, country to city. It is likely that this revaluation was influenced by Lenin. In Two Tactics of Social-Democracy (1905) Lenin called the Bolsheviks the 'Jacobins of contemporary Social-Democracy' whose slogan is 'the revolutionary-democratic dictatorship of the proletariat and peasantry'. In July 1917 he wrote : ' "Jacobinism" in Europe or on the bound ary line between Europe and Asia in the twentieth century would be the rule of the revolutionary class, of the which, supported by the peasant poor and taking advantage of the existing material basis for the advance to socialism, could not only provide all the great, unforgettable things provided by the Jacobins in the eighteenth century but bring about a lasting world-wide victory for the work ing people .'

## National-popular

This term is associated with the concepts of hegemony and Jacobinism as well as being a recurrent term in Gramsci's cultural analyses. Politically, a national-popular movement is one in which a fundamental class becomes hegemonic at a national level by drawing subaltern social groups into an alliance. 'Any formation of a national-popular collective will is impossible unless the great mass of peasant farmers bursts simultaneously into political life.' (SPN 132) The term 'nation al-popular' reflects Gramsci's conception of the revolution in Italy as a national movement which fulfils under socialism the historical tasks which the bourgeoisie had abdicated after the Risorgimento. As he had written in 1919: 'Historically the bourgeois class is already dead . . . Today the "national" class is the proletariat.' (L'Ordine Nuovo, 1919- 1920 , Turin 1975 , p. 278) . Culturally, the term (which was perhaps influenced by nineteenth-century Russian debates) designates forms of art and literature which help cement this kind of hegemonic alliance: neither ' intellectualistic' nor 'cosmopolitan' but engaging with popular reality audiences. Italian intellectuals are and drawing in popular historically non-national popular (see XII.l, 'Concept of "National-Popular" ') .

'Organic' and 'conjunctural'

For Gramsci , Marxist analysis must distinguish what is organic, that is to say of the whole system and relatively permanent , from what is conjunctural , that is to say specific to a given moment. It must know how to read the structural contradictions in the economy beneath the conjunctural conflicts at the level of the political system and of ideology . Gramsci 's position here is different from that of economism (q .v.) with which it might at first sight be confused . For the latter, one must always look to the 'reality' of the economic base beneath the 'appearances' of the superstructures. For Gramsci, on the other hand, one must constantly connect the organic and the conjunctural moments to one another. This means understanding and seeing as equally real the terrain of the conjunctural since it is precisely 'upon this terrain that the forces of opposition organize'. The error comes when one pays excessive attention only to one or the other. Overemphasis on the organic at the expense of the conjunctural leads to economism, just as an overemphasis on the conjunctural leads to 'ideologism'. (See VI . IO).

## Organic crisis

An 'organic crisis' is a crisis of the whole system in which contradictions in the economic structure have repercussions through the superstructures. One of its signs is when the traditional forms of political representation (parties or party leaders) are no longer recognized as adequate by the economic class or class fraction which they had previously served to represent. It is therefore a crisis of hegemony since it occurs when a formerly hegemonic class is challenged from below and is no longer able to hold together a cohesive bloc of social alliances. Such an organic crisis opened, in Gramsci's analysis, in Italy before the First World War, when the bourgeoisie and the landowners, faced with the growing power of working-class organizations, lost confidence in the Liberal ruling elite to represent them. Organic crises produce a situation of rapid political realignments. In Italy after the war, these resulted in the rise to power of Fascism. (See VI.1 2 and VIII.9 and 10).

## Passive revolution

Gramsci adapts the term 'passive revolution' from Vincenzo Cuoco 's history of the 1799 revolution in Naples, but it is 'completely modified' by his own usage (Q 15§17, p. 1775) . It is used to describe any historical situation in which a new political formation comes to power without a fundamental reordering of social relations. He first applies it to the Risorgimento to describe the process by which the bourgeoisie represented by Cavou(s Moderates , achieves power without a revolution of the French type. He then extends it to other liberal movements of the post-1815 restoration and finally to fascism, which modernizes the economy 'from above' by breaking the political power of both the laissez-faire bourgeoisie and the organised working class . Gramsci describes these forms of passive revolution as manifestations of a 'war of position' by the dominant classes after a phase of the war of manoeuvre from below (French Revolution; the period 19 17-21) . Although it has sometimes been asserted - perhaps because of this assimilation between passive revolution and war of position - that Gramsci also advocated a form of 'passive revolution' for the left, in fact he explicitly says that it is only an analytical tool, a 'criterion of interpretation', and not a programme 'as i t was for the Italian liberals of the Risorgimento' (VIII.5). He also say s that the 'dialectic of conservation and innovation' which constitutes passive revolution 'is called reformism ' in modern terminology (Q10 11 §41. xiv , p. 1325) . See in particular Section VIII .

## *Philosophy of praxis*

This term is used in many passages of the prison notebooks in place of Marxism ( Gramsci also refers to Marx as 'the founder of the philosophy of praxis' and to Lenin as 'the greatest modern theorist of the philosophy of praxis' : VI .6) . The expression , however, is more than a device to bypass the censor: it also conveys (as it did for the Socialist philosopher Antonio Labriola from whom Gramsci borrowed it) a specific conception of Marxism as a unity of theory and practice. For Gramsci the philosophy of praxis is both the theory of the contradictions in society and at the same time people's practical awareness of those contradictions. The philosophy of praxis is the 'self-consciousness' of historical 'necessity'. It involves the formation of a revolutionary collective will which can act in accordance with that necessity. Gramsci in other words, sees the philosophy of praxis not only as a system of philosophical ideas but also as forming the basis of a mass 'conception of the world' : 'the character of the philosophy of praxis is especially that of being a mass conception, a mass culture, that of a mass which operates as a unit, in other words one which has norms of conduct which are not only universal a t the level of ideas, but "generalized" in social reality. ' (Q IO, II§3 1)

'The philosophy of praxis is absolute "historicism" , the absolute bringing down to earth and worldliness of thought, an absolute humanism of history. Along this line, one must trace the thread of the new conception of the world.' (Q 11§27 , SPN 465 , translation slightly altered) .

State

Gramsci uses the term 'state ' in at least two different senses in the prison notebooks. In the first (n arrow) sense the state is a sphere of 'domination', the organ or instrument of the oppression of one class by another (see , for instance, X. I, p. 306) . This corresponds to one of the uses of the term in Marx and to Lenin's use in Th e State and Revolution and it was also the main sense in which the term was used in the Second and Third Internationals. In the second (wider) sense (which seems also to be a later one in the composition of the notebooks) the state is an 'integral' state . It has the functions both of coercion and of consent. It contains both the apparatuses of government and the judiciary and the various voluntary and private associations and para-political institutions which make up civil society (q.v.). In this wider sense, the state possesses 'educative' and 'ethical' functions which will remain, indeed expand, under socialism as the state in the narrow sense (as an instrument of coercion and class domination) withers away 'It is possible to imagine the coercive element of the state withering away by degrees, as ever more conspicuous elements of regulated society (or ethical state or civil society) make their appearance.' (VII.8) Within the integral state, the term civil society has 'the sense of the political and cultural hegemony of a social group over the whole of society, the ethical content of the state' (Q6§24 , p. 703 , my italics . In the first sense, then, state is separated from civil society, as coercion against consent, domination against direction, and dictatorship against hegemony. In the second sense, state includes both civil society and the state in the first or narrow sense (now called 'political society') . In both cases the distinction between two 'regions' (political society/civil society) is the same, and both together are methodologically separated by Gramsci from a third 'region' - 'economic society' or the economic structure.

## Transformism.

A term originally used in Italian political jargon in the late 1870s to describe loose alliances between factions of Left and Right (opponents were 'transformed' into supporters across the floor of parliament), Gramsci extends it to describe the characteristic form of bourgeois hegemony in Italy between unification and Fascism. With a system of transformism, there is no real opposition or alternation in power. Instead, there is a piecemeal absorption of the opposition by the ruling elites. Gramsci distinguishes two main phases: 1860-1900, 'molecular' transformism, in which individual exponents of the democratic opposition go over to the moderate-conservative centre; 1900- 1918, transformism of whole groups of the left who go over to the centre or right : for instance, the Nationalist party is formed out of ex- anarchists and syndicalists (Q8§36 , pp . 962-63).

War of Manoeuvre/War of Position

These military terms, used in relation to the First World War, meant , respectively , a war of rapid movement with a series of frontal assaults , and trench warfare backed up by reserves of supplies, munitions and soldiers behind the lines. In parallel with the state/civil society distinction, Gramsci applies the two concepts to politics.

'It seems to me that Ilyich [Lenin] understood that a change was necessary from a war of manoeuvre [frontal attack on the state] applied victoriously in the East in 1917, to a war of position which was the only form possible in the West.' (VII .2)

War of position is linked to Gramsci's notion of hegemony in its various senses: class alliances, 'molecular' ideological and political work in civil society, consent. It should be noted, however, that he uses the term 'war of position ' not only to designate a revolutionary strategy for the left but also to describe a phase of 'revolution-reaction' or passive revolution (q.v.) which follows upon a revolutionary offensive (war of manoeuvre) : in this sense fascism is also a form of war of position (see p. 267) .

Gramsci, Antonio; Forgacs, David. The Antonio Gramsci Reader: Selected Writings 1916-1935 (pp. 646-654). New York University Press. Kindle Edition.

**Bibliography.**

Primary Sources:

Bloomfield, Robert (1916) Poems: a collection [ unknown].
Bloomfield, Robert (1947) A Selection of Poems, London, The Grey Wall Press.
Bloomfield, Robert (2007) Selected Poems, Nottingham, Nottingham Trent University.
Byron. English Bards, and Scotch Reviewers: A Satire. (Kindle Locations 640-644). Printed for James Cawthorn. Kindle Edition.
Clare, John...
1. Poems descriptive of rural life and scenery (London, 1820).
2. The village minstrel and other poems [2v.] (London, 1821).
3. The shepherd's calendar: with village stories and other poems (London, 1827).
4. The rural muse: poems (London, 1835).
5. Life and remains of John Clare: the Northamptonshire peasant poet, by J.L. Cherry (London, 1873).
6. Poems, ed. with an introduction by Arthur Symons (London, 1908).
7. Poems, chiefly from the manuscript, ed. by Edmund Blunden and Alan Porter (London, 1920)
8. Madrigals and chronicles, being newly found poems written by John Clare, ed. with a preface and commentary by Edmund Blunden (London, 1924).
9. Sketches in the life of John Clare, written by himself, now first published, with an introduction,

notes, and additions by Edmund Blunden (London, 1931).
10. The poems of John Clare, ed. with an introduction by J.W. Tibble [2v.] (London, 1935).
11. Poems of John Clare's madness, ed. with an introduction by Geoffrey Grigson (London, 1949).
12. The letters of John Clare, ed. by J.W. and A. Tibble (London, 1951).
13. The prose of John Clare, ed. by J.W. and A. Tibble (London, 1951).
14. Selected letters, ed. by Mark Storey (Oxford, 1988).
15. The early poems of John Clare: 1804-1822, general ed. Eric Robinson [2v.] (Oxford, 1989).
16. Poems of the middle period, 1822-1837, general ed. Eric Robinson [4v.] (Oxford, 1996-98).
17. Poems of the middle period, 1822-1837, Volume V, general ed. Eric Robinson (Oxford, 2003).
18. Poems of the Later Period (1964) eds Eric Robinson & Geoffrey Summerfield.
19. Clare, John (2013) [ed] Storey, The Critical Heritage. New York, Routledge.
Mew, Charlotte "The Trees are Down" from Collected Poems and Prose (Manchester, England: Carcanet Press Ltd., 1981).
https://www.poetryfoundation.org/poems/51731/the-trees-are-down
 Southey, Robert (1836) The Works and Lives of the Uneducated Poets.
Wordsworth, William (2008) William Wordsworth, The Major Works, Oxford, Oxford University Press.
Yearsley, Ann (1931) Poems On Several Occasions, London, Scholar Select.

Yearsley, Ann (1787) Poems on various subjects by Ann Yearsley…being her second collection. British Museum, Ecco Print.

Yearsley, Ann (2003) Selected Poems, University of Gloucestershire, The Cyder Press.

## Secondary Sources:

Althusser, Louis (1971) For Marx, London, Allen Lane Penguin Press.
Althusser, Louis, Ideological State Apparatus Louis Althusser Ideology And Ideological State Apparatuses (Notes ...
Anderson, Perry (1976) Considerations on Western Marxism
Perry Anderson : Considerations On Western Marxism (1976)
Anderson, Perry (2020) The Antinomies of Antonio Gramsci. London, Verso.
Andrews, Kerry (2015) Ann Yearsley and Hannah More, Patronage and Poetry Routledge, London.
Bate, Johnathan (2004) John Clare, London. Picador.
Clare, Johanne (1987) John Clare and the Bounds of Circumstance, Kingston, McGill Queen's University Press.
Callinicos, Alex, (2021), The Routledge Handbook on Marxism and Post Marxism, London, Routledge.
Caudwell, Christopher (1946) Illusion and Reality, London, Lawrence, and Wishart.
Empson, Martin (2022), Socialism or Extinction, London, Bookmarks.
Gramsci, Antonio (1971) Selections from Prison Notebooks. London, Lawrence & Wishart.
Gramsci, Antonio (1999) The Antonio Gramsci Reader, London, Lawrence & Wishart.
Gramsci, Antonio in Alfonso Bordello (2020) Gramsci: Introduction, Villaggio Publishing Ltd. Kindle Edition., p. 5.

Hall, Stuart (1981) Notes on deconstructing the popular, in R. Samuel (ed) People's History and Socialist History, London, Routledge.

Hall, Stuart with A. Bailey (1992) Cultural studies and its theoretical legacies, in Culture Studies, New York, Routledge.

Harman, Chris, "Gramsci, the Prison Notebooks and Philosophy", International Socialism 114 (spring 2007).

John Clare in Context (1994) Hugh Haughton (Editor), Adam Phillips (Editor), Geoffrey Summerfield (Editor), Cambridge, Cambridge University Press.

https://www.historicalmaterialism.org/blog/intellectuals

Lenin (1901/1902). What is to be Done? https://www.marxists.org/archive/lenin/works/1901/witbd

Lodge, S Clare, John Clare 1793-1864, ProQuest, Ann Arbor.

James C. McKusick, John Clare, and the Tyranny of Grammar
https://www.proquest.com/docview/1297400775?parentSessionId=IEQIDHCnQfQcGqALrfFV1ZgCW%2Fbyij5SiexVc291JTw%3D&pq-origsite=primo&accountid=14697

Landry, Donna (1990) The Muses of Resistance: Labouring Class Women's Poetry in Britain 1739-1796, Cambridge, Cambridge University Press.

Marx, Karl & Engels Frederick (1848) Communist Manifesto

Manifesto of the Communist Party - Marxists

Marx Karl (1859) Preface to A Contribution to the Critique of Political Economy):

https://www.marxists.org/archive/marx/works/1859/critique-pol-economy/preface.htm
Marx & Engels The German Ideology The German Ideology - Marxists
Molyneux, John (2021) The Dialectics of Art, London, Haymarket.
Molyneux, John (2022) Selected Works: Essays on Socialism and Revolution. London, Bookmarks.
Paulin, Tom (1992) Minotaur: Poetry and the Nation State, London, Faber & Faber.
Paulin, Tom in Guyer, Sara (2015), Reading with John Clare, Biopoetics, Sovereignty, Romanticism (Lit Z) I, USA, Fordham University Press.
Schwarzmantel, John. (2015) The Routledge Guidebook to Gramsci's Prison Notebooks, Taylor, and Francis. Kindle Edition.
Storey, Mark (1974) The Poetry of John Clare: A Critical Introduction. New York MacMillian.
Thomas, P D (2009, The Gramscian Moment, London, Haymarket.
Thompson, E. P (1968) The Making of the English Working Class, revised. Harmondsworth: Pelican Books.
Trotsky (1924) https://www.marxists.org/archive/trotsky/1924/lit_revo/ch08.htm
Vardy, Alan (2003) John Clare, Politics and Poetry, New York, Palgrave MacMillian.
Waldron, Mary (1996) Lactila, Milkmaid of Clifton: The Life and Writings of Ann Yearsley, USA, University of Georgia Press.
White, Simon (2016) Robert Bloomfield, Romanticism and the Poetry of Community, London, Routledge.

Williams, Raymond (1977) Marxism and Literature. Oxford, Oxford University Press.

New Woman' and Hobgoblins: The Communist Manifesto in 19th-Century Britain and its literary aftermaths. A Study of Helen Macfarlane and Eleanor Marx.

## Positional Quotes.

'A spectre is haunting Europe – the spectre of communism.'
- Communist Manifesto, as translated by Samuel Moore in cooperation with Engels, - 1888.

'A frightful hobgoblin stalks throughout Europe. We are haunted by a ghost, the ghost of Communism.'
- Manifesto of the German Communist Party, translated by
  Helen Macfarlane, 1850.

'Women are the creatures of an organised tyranny of men, as the workers are the creatures of an organised tyranny of idlers … But the one [woman] has nothing to hope from man, and the other [the worker] has nothing to hope from the middle class.'
- The Women Question from a Socialist Point of View, Eleanor
  Marx & Edward Aveling 1886.

'If women's liberation is unthinkable without Communism, then Communism is unthinkable without women's liberation.'
  - Inessa Armand quoted in Sharon Smith Women and Socialism (Illinois, Haymarket Books (2015).

. 'But reality can be seized and penetrated only as a totality, and only a subject which itself is a totality is capable of this penetration.'
- Lukács, Georg History and Class Consciousness.

'The proletariat cannot liberate itself as a class without simultaneously abolishing class society as such. For that reason, its consciousness, the last class consciousness in the history of mankind, must both lay bare the nature of society and achieve an increasingly inward fusion of theory and practice.'
- Lukács, History and Class Consciousness.

'... If ideology were merely some abstract, imposed set of notions, if our social and political and cultural ideas and assumptions and habits were merely the result of specific manipulation, of a kind of overt training which might be simply ended or withdrawn, then the society would be very much easier to move and to change than in practice it has ever been or is. '
- Raymond Williams Problems of Materialism (London, Verso 1980).

This thesis is of significance because it illuminates an important 'hidden history' of 19th-century 'New Woman' on the British Left employing the methodology of Marxism and its sister models as they developed across time until the late 20th century and into the 21st. It will explore recent studies of Helen Macfarlane and Eleanor Marx, their lives and writing and analyse them from a theoretical perspective rather than understanding them simply as historical figures. It will, therefore, attempt a dialectical synthesis of these elements. Thus, recognising the importance of the 'personal as political' but transcending that biographical category and understanding the fusion of Labour & literature. These two women will be shown, like Karl Marx and Frederick Engels, to have been polymaths and will attempt to delineate their demise employing the living tradition in which they had fought for socialism. This thesis will make a connection in terms of Althusserian problematics and concomitant symptomatic readings between the suicides of Eleanor Marx and Sylvia Plath. It will endeavour to further the knowledge of an internationalist and revolutionist tradition within Britain and ask why these two women leaders were almost lost to the modern scholar. I will employ the ideas of Marx, Engels, Luxemburg, Trotsky, Kollontai, Lukács, Althusser and Gramsci as the main structure for this analysis. However, I will also illustrate the impact of modern feminism from Simone de Beauvoir, Kate Millet, Elaine Schowalter, Lise Vogel and then 21st century Marxist feminists Sharon Smith and Judith Orr in reaching my conclusion. That in 'the last instant' women's oppression can only be resolved in a qualitatively different society. Thus, Lukács insight that this would be 'the-identical-subject-object of history', socialism. Helen Macfarlane and Eleanor Marx will be shown to be the equals of the intellectually advanced elements of the British, the international Left. I shall argue they were oppressed by patriarchy and capitalism.

## Contents

Introduction.

Soundings.

Thesis and methodology. Marx and Engels in Britain during the 1840s and Chartism. Communist Manifesto and its Histories. a) Relationship to The League of the Just. b) Engels' early drafts c) An evolution of Prefaces.

Chapter One.

## Kant and Hegel in Britain.

Helen Macfarlane and her translations of Hegel, the Communist Manifesto and other writings including critiques of Carlyle and literary texts. Conclusion: Utopian-Socialism, not Scientific Socialism, somewhat akin to George Elliot's translation of Strauss and Feuerbach and that milieu. No evidence that the two met but were published in contending London papers The Leader & Red Republican. There is textual material to suggest that Elliot thought Macfarlane too radical. Interestingly they both returned to the dominant ideology of their epoch, Christianity in one way or another.


Chapter Two.

## Death and Resurrection in Nantwich.

Helen Macfarlane's Legacy. Personal tragedies then married a vicar, but the seeds were already there in her earlier written works. So consistent Utopian Socialist /Bourgeois Idealist.

## Chapter Three.

### Eleanor Marx: A Dreamer of Absolutes.

A 'new wave' of proletarian struggle: the Paris Commune 1870, she writes Shelley's Socialism. Bloody Sunday in London, 1880's. Eleanor Marx as the embodiment of Marxist 'praxis'. Conflict with Althusserian R.S.A.

## Chapter Four.

Ibsen's Doll's House. A Study in Patriarchy.

Eleanor Marx was the victim of being unconsciously interpellated by Patriarchy so although able to lead worker's' movements she was unable to defy Edward Aveling sexist behaviour and when the class struggle waned her only consolation was the grave. The Althusserian problematic of the epoch would not be answered by the Paris Commune. The silences could only be answered with the symptomatic reading of the narrative that began in 1917. Too late for Eleanor Marx. Eleanor Marx and Aveling claimed to be Ibsenites. At the first English reading of A Doll's House given in their Chancery Lane lodgings in 1886. Eleanor read Nora, Aveling (portentously) Helmer and Bernard Shaw, Krogstad.

Chapter Five.

Hot Autumn: Alexandra Kollontai, the Doll's House Unlocked.

Kollontai in the context of the early Russian revolution provided the key to unlock the Doll's House. The Stalinist counter-revolution locked it again.

Conjectures and Reawakening:

Simone de Beauvoir, The Second Sex.
Kate Millet, Sexual Politics,
Elaine Showalter, A Literature of Their Own.
Lise Vogel, Marxism, and the Oppression of Women: Towards a Unitary Theory.
Sharon Smith, Women and Socialism.
Judith Orr, Marxism and Women's Liberation.


Conclusion:

Both Helen Macfarlane and Eleanor Marx were committed, revolutionary socialists. Both in leadership roles. However, in terms of their belief systems, they failed. Helen 'sold out.' Eleanor committed suicide. In The Myth of Sisyphus Albert Camus argued: 'The consequences of realization are suicide or recovery.' For these two revolutionaries to have stood on the peaks of class struggle and seen it evaporate would have been overwhelming. Helen Macfarlane sought solace in illusion, her alienated species - being (Feuerbach/Marx/ Freud) religion buried at St.

Michael's Church, Baddeley, just outside Nantwich. 'Tussey', ever the active agent, (her motto: 'Always ahead') took her own life, I suggest because, in the 'last instant' her life was revolution and literature and thus because of the downturn in class-struggle and the rise of Aestheticism there was no hope. These women, although significant figures on the Left, were doubly oppressed, by Capital and Patriarchy. I thus, find a degree of explanatory value in 'dual systems theory' school of socialist – feminism. However, a solution can only be found when the proletariat acts as a 'class-for-itself' and becomes what Lukács, called, the 'identical-subject-object of history.' As Trotsky noted this is neither a mechanistic nor voluntarist process:

The progress of a class toward class consciousness, that is, the building of a revolutionary party which leads the proletariat is a complex and a contradictory process. The class itself is not homogeneous. Its different sections arrive at class consciousness by different paths and at different times.

## Appendix A/B.

Introduction:
Soundings.

This thesis I maintain is of significance because it illuminates an important 'hidden history' of 19th-century women on the British Left. Their writing and their lives. I will argue that there was little or no intellectual division of labour in the leadership of the Radical Left in nineteenth-century Britain. They were polymaths. So, Marx had been a poet, philosopher, literary critic, and economist as well as his political activities. Although this was replicated in both Helen Macfarlane and Eleanor Marx their outcomes were very different from their male counterparts. This begs the question, why? Thus, this thesis is concerned with two leading women figures, the dialectical relationship between their writing and life within the radical left in nineteenth-century Britain. They were not marginalised in their epoch, held leadership roles but became almost lost to the modern reader. My argument is that in order to comprehend this experience a rigorous theoretical structure is necessary, thus a literary material praxis.

To return to a quintessential current which runs through my argument is that for those around the leadership on the radical Left in Britain, and later abroad, there was not a division of mental labour between writing and reading of diverse non-fictional and the fictional, the literary. This is exemplified in an eminent study of Karl Marx's reading by S. S. Prawer Karl Marx and World Literature . Although I disagree with Prawer when

he describes Marx as 'dancing on the superstructure.'. An early love of Karl Marx's had been Prometheus:
Prometheus is the foremost saint and martyr in the philosopher's calendar.

More significant still was Eleanor Marx's remark that her father: 'was a unique and unrivalled storyteller'. As a young man influenced by those two giants of German Romanticism, Goethe and Schiller, Marx wrote poetry. However, Karl Marx soon rejected 'German Romantic dreaming' for his own Materialist 'reality principle' (Prawer, 2015, p. 17). Marx's 'reality principle' would, of course, develop into a fully-fledged metanarrative held together not by Stalinist heroes nor the exegesis of the precise meaning of this or that text. For as Marx himself famously said: 'I am not a Marxist'. This phrase occurred in a letter of 1890 from Engels to C. Schmidt in Stuttgart in which he recollected Marx's phrase that followed a controversy shortly before Marx died. Marx had written a letter to Eleanor's sister's partner Paul Lafarge and Jules Guesde London, August 5th, 1883 both of whom already claimed to represent "Marxist" principles. Marx accused them of "revolutionary phrase-mongering". Engels continued in the same letter to Schmidt:
According to the materialist conception of history for a lot of them nowadays, it serves as an excuse for not studying history just as Marx used to say, commenting on the French "Marxists" of the late seventies: "All I know is that I am not a Marxist."

In my search for a method, György Lukács' study into the nature of Marxist dialectics is an invaluable steppingstone although this thesis will also explore the thinking of Louis Althusser and I will note a tension between their perspectives. The former may be described as a 'humanist' reading of 'Hegelian Marxism" and the latter a 'structural' Marxism originating in Semiotics. A third innovatory Marxist thinker, Trotsky, will contribute. All are valuable tools in elucidating 'hidden histories'.

and the nature of capitalism. Here Lukács is persuasive:

Let us assume for the sake of argument that recent research had disproved once and for all every one of Marx's individual theses… Orthodox Marxism, therefore, does not imply the uncritical acceptance of the results of Marx's investigations. It is not the 'belief' in this or that thesis, nor the exegesis of a 'sacred' book. On the contrary, orthodoxy refers exclusively to method. Therefore, I am interested in Dialectical Materialism as a method. Firstly, the transformation from a quantitative to a qualitative condition, thus producing a new state and secondly Interdependent material opposites which are by nature antagonistic, finally 'the negation of the negation' which creates a new thesis afresh with elements of the old but also completely new material. I will delineate two core concepts: 1) the Marxist dialectic [Karl Marx never used the term dialectical materialism]. Engels described it persuasively in Dialectics of Nature: Dialectics (The general nature of dialectics to be developed …in contrast to metaphysics) and 2) Historical

Materialism. I note that Georg Lukacs did not follow Engels position in Dialectics of Nature when they were applied to ahistorical phenomena. However, I agree with the school of thought which understands Marxism as a 'living tradition' not as an ossified one as here in Rosa Luxemburg:

Marxism is a revolutionary worldview that must always struggle for new revelations. Marxism must abhor nothing so much as the possibility that it becomes congealed in its current form. It is at its best when butting heads in self-criticism, and in historical thunder and lightning, it retains its strength.

I shall look at the antecedents of The Communist Manifesto beginning with Engels contact with the Chartists and its histories. Then a) Relationship to The Communist League, b) Engels' drafts of The Principles of Communism, 1847, c) The Communist Manifesto by Marx & Engels, 1848 d) Helen Macfarlane's 1850 translation, e) evolution of Prefaces by Marx & Engels from 1872 through to Engels' last Italian preface of 1893 in which he makes an allusion to a new Dante for the next century.

## Chapter One.

Kant and Hegel in Britain.

David Black, a Libertarian Socialist did much to resurrect the figure of Helen Macfarlane in Helen Macfarlane Red Republican and Helen Macfarlane A Feminist, Revolutionary Journalist, and Philosopher in Mid-Nineteenth- Century England . While Louise Yeoman, a BBC historian has also contributed valuable information. The seeds or contradictions within Helen Macfarlane which led her to move towards Christianity from Left Radicalism were not simply precipitated by the premature and tragic loss of her husband and child. Her consequent marriage to a vicar had its origins in her writings as a radical in 1850. At that time, she was associated with Marx and Engels as well as Ernest Jones and Julian Harney. I will endeavour to show how her translation of the Communist Manifesto was not 'a somewhat fanciful version' as was claimed by David MacLellan The Communist Manifesto. Rather it was a work of poetic imagination that was congruent with its host publications the Democratic Review 1849-1850 and the Red Republican and its aspirations which included the publication of poetry. It is significant that David Black uncovered the fact that Heaney cut parts of Helen Macfarlane's translation of the Communist Manifesto in Red Republican. However, Black does not provide a convincing reason for this censorship. Unlike most of the leadership of Leftist ''the Charter and something more' Heaney had been a proletarian autodidact and experienced agitator [see Foot, Paul The Vote (London, Bookmarks, 2006) pp 89-90.

Engels first contact with the Chartists was in 1842 when he visited the offices of The Northern Star. In June 1847 Marx & Engels tentatively joined the League of the Just a largely German Utopian/Christian-communist secret organisation who had believed, initially, in the establishment of 'the kingdom of God on Earth' through revolution or b) utopian commune in America, c) the establishment of worker stock-companies in France & Germany. Marx/Engels were invited to join this somewhat disparate clandestine group. Marx & Engels won the argument after debates culminating in the 10-day First Congress of the Communist League. However, some of the members of the organization persisted in conspiratorial and utopian stances and it was only after the Second Congress in Autumn 1847 that a recognizable Marxist line was accepted both in theory and practice and the group rejected clandestine activity. Consequently, they asked Marx & Engels to write a political programme. Engels begun work on a document which was a catechism entitled The Principles of Communism in December 1847. However, he was dissatisfied with the document and asked Marx to write a more historical document. As always Marx struggled with focusing on one task at a time but after the Communist League threatened disciplinary action Marx completed the Communist Manifesto in eight weeks in 1848.

Marx & Engels wrote in the in 1872 Preface to German edition "It was published in English for the first time in 1850 in the Red Republican, London, translated by Miss Helen Macfarlane." Marx & Engel speculated in the 1882 Preface to the Russian edition 'Now the question is: can the Russian obshchina [village commune], though greatly undermined, yet a form of primeval common ownership of land, pass directly to the higher form of Communist common ownership? Or, on the contrary, must it first pass through the same process of such as constitutes the historical evolution of the West? The only answer to that possible today is this: If the Russian Revolution becomes the signal for a proletarian revolution in the West, so that both complement each other, the present Russian common ownership of land may serve as the starting point for a communist development.

Engels wrote in 1883 Preface to the German Edition [ just after Marx's death on March 14, 1883] 'the basic thought running through the Manifesto remains solely and exclusively with Marx.'.
In the 1888 Preface to the English edition which became the Standard English Language Version Engels concluded: 'The present translation is by Mr Samuel Moore, the translator of the greater portion of Marx' s Capital. We have revised it in common, and I have added a few notes explanatory of historical allusions.'

Engels concludes the last Preface he penned in the 1893 Italian edition: 'Today, as in 1300, a new historical era is approaching. Will Italy give us the new Dante, who will mark the hour of birth of this new, proletarian era?'

The Communist Manifesto contains four sections. The Communist Manifesto is divided into a preamble and four sections, the last of these a short conclusion. The introduction of the 1888 authorized Samuel Moore/ Engels begins by proclaiming: "A spectre is haunting Europe—the spectre of communism. All the powers of old Europe have entered into a holy alliance to exorcise this spectre". Pointing out that parties everywhere—including those in government and those in the opposition—have flung the "branding reproach of communism" at each other, the authors infer from this that the powers-that-be acknowledge communism to be a power in itself. Subsequently, the introduction exhorts Communists to openly publish their views and aims, to "meet this nursery tale of the spectre of communism with a manifesto of the party itself". The first section of the Manifesto, "Bourgeois and Proletarians", elucidates the materialist conception of history, that "the history of all hitherto existing society is the history of class struggles". Societies have always taken the form of an oppressed majority exploited under the yoke of an oppressive minority. In capitalism, the industrial working class, or proletariat, engage in class struggle against the owners of the means of production, the bourgeoisie. As before, this struggle will end in a revolution that restructures society, or the "common ruin of the contending classes". The bourgeoisie, through the "constant revolutionising of production [and] uninterrupted disturbance of all social conditions" have emerged as the supreme class in society, displacing all the old powers of feudalism. The bourgeoisie constantly exploits the proletariat for its labour power, creating profit for themselves and accumulating capital. However, in doing so the bourgeoisie serves as "its own grave-diggers"; the proletariat inevitably will become conscious of their own potential and rise to power through revolution, overthrowing the bourgeoisie. "Proletarians and Communists", the second section, starts by stating the relationship of conscious communists to the rest of the working class. The communists' party will not oppose other working-class parties, but unlike them, it will express the general will and defend the common interests of the world's proletariat as a whole, independent of all nationalities. The section goes on to defend communism from various objections, including claims that it advocates communal prostitution or disincentivises people from working. The third section, "Socialist and Communist Literature", distinguishes communism from other socialist doctrines prevalent at the time—these being broadly categorised as Reactionary Socialism; Conservative or Bourgeois Socialism; and Critical-Utopian Socialism and Communism. While the degree of reproach toward rival perspectives varies, all are dismissed for advocating reformism and failing to recognise the pre-eminent revolutionary role of the working class.

"Position of the Communists in Relation to the Various Opposition Parties", the concluding section of the Manifesto, briefly discusses the communist position on struggles in specific countries in the mid-nineteenth century such as France, Switzerland, Poland and Germany, this last being "on the eve of a bourgeois revolution" and predicts that a world revolution will soon follow. It ends by declaring an alliance with the democratic socialists, boldly supporting other communist revolutions and calling for united international proletarian action—"Working Men of All Countries, Unite!".

Helen Macfarlane's 1850 translation is far more poetic using metaphors:

'A frightful hobgoblin stalks throughout Europe. We are haunted by the ghost, the ghost of communism. Macfarlane, David Black notes, uses the language of Hamlet and Scottish folklore. I would argue the first metaphor also rests on her knowledge of Kantian philosophy i.e. the differentiation between the Phenomenological world and the noumenal world or 'things-in-themselves'. We can also note the creative use of metre and repetition.

'Shopocracy' for the petty bourgeoisie. An imaginative Anglicisation which would resonant with British workers.

'Proletarians of the world unite.' Is gender neutral unlike Samuel Moore's 'Working men of the world unite.'

## Helen Macfarlane.

Influenced by the German philosophy of Kant and Hegel.
Kant on 'the synthetic a priori' in A Critique of Pure Reason that he wrote as a response to reading David Hume in translation. At the time, the 18th century, Western thought was divided between Idealists or Rationalists who believed you could know about something through thought or Reason [knowledge of things without empirical proof they existed] like Descartes: 'Cogito Ergo Sum' = 'I think therefore I am' and those who thought you could not such as the Empiricists in Britain like John Locke and David Hume. Who contested that you could not have a priori knowledge but rather believed we are born 'Tableau rasa' = 'a blank slate'. Kant attempted to move beyond these competing positions and argued we can know the world 'Synthetic a priori'. To explain this, we need to first understand he thought there was a difference between the 1) the phenomenological world i.e. what we see and 2) the noumenal world which lies beyond appearances. Thus, he had a gap which he attempted to explain. Therefore, some things, he argued, are 'true by definition' or 'Analytic' to use his term e.g., 'men are male' and 'mammals suckle their young.' This type of knowledge we can know without experience by reason or thought in a sentence. Others again to employ Kant's term are 'Synthetic' and requires observation and experience such as 'all lemons are bitter' is based on empirical data he argued. Thus, his 'breakthrough' was some are 'Synthetic a priori' like 7+5=12 which he claimed we can

know by new knowledge. Knowledge about the world by thinking about it. It is a 'Synthetic statement' arrived at by thought which we did not need to check against observation of the world. Helen Macfarlane, I have suggested, employed her knowledge of Kantian philosophy and applies it to Scottish folklore in the opening line of The Communist Manifesto to create the metaphor i.e. an image within Kant's noumenal world which lies beyond appearances i.e. Hobgoblin 'A frightful hobgoblin stalks throughout Europe'.(Black [ed] 2014 p.119).

David Black (2004) p.96 argues that the hobgoblin was both a ghostly apparition emanating from Hamlet and Scottish folklore.
Helen Macfarlane concludes her 1850 translation of the Communist Manifesto with 'Let the Proletarians of the world unite.' (ibid, p149) which is a literal translation. While Samuel Moore advised by Engels concluded their English version in 1888 with 'WORKING MEN OF ALL COUNTRIES, UNITE!". This translation is the authorised translation by Engels and is the most commonly used version in English. We can see that Macfarlane was more accurate but also did not employ the Patriarchal language of Moore, she thus remained closer to Marx's original text. Macfarlane termed the poetic term 'Shopocracy rather than the usual 'petty bourgeois.'
Macfarlane engaged with other issues of her day. Her first published article in Democratic Review, a theoretical journal, in April 1850 was an attack on Thomas Carlyle.

Macfarlane and Hegel. Macfarlane had not 'turned Hegel on his head' as Marx had done:
The mystification which the dialectic suffers in Hegel's hands by no means prevents him from presenting its general forms of motion in a comprehensive and conscious manner. With him it is sitting on its head. It must be inverted, in order to discover the rational kernel within the mystical shell.

Rather in Macfarlane's thought we can comprehend the philosophical basis in Kant and Hegel for her later retreat from Radical or Scientific Socialism to Anglicanism
Democracy, the Idea of the 19th century, is a great and most welcome fact. This idea has revealed itself at different times, and in different ways. I find it has assumed four forms, which, at first sight, are very unlike each other, yet they are only different ways of expressing the same thing, or, to speak strictly, they are the necessary moments in the development, or unfolding, of the idea: and the last of these forms presupposes the foregoing ones – as the fruit presupposes the flower, and that again, the bud. These forms are, the religion taught by the divine Galilean Republican – the reformation of the 16th century – the German philosophy from Emmanuel Kant to Hegel, and the Democracy of our own times.
She was understanding History as the self-conscious unfolding of the Idea as a Hegelian. However, if the Idea was not inverted and given a dialectical materialist grounding, then when the class struggle ebbed the step to an immanent pantheism was the next phase. The embracing of

a transcendent God although not inevitable was, in the climate of defeat, understandable.

## Julian Harney and Macfarlane, the break and beyond.

### Fraternal Democrats.

Fraternal Democrats was an international society, founded at a meeting held in London on September 22. 1845. The society embraced representatives of Left Chartists, German workers, and craftsmen – members of the League of the Just – and revolutionary emigrants of other nationalities. During their stay in England in the summer of 1845, Karl Marx and Friedrich Engels helped in preparing for the meeting but did not attend it as they had by then left London. Later they kept in constant touch with the Fraternal Democrats trying to influence the proletarian core of the society, which joined the Communist League in 1847, and through it the Chartist movement. The society ceased its activities in 1853.

After the failure of revolutions of 1848 Engels claimed, 'the revolution would only be consummated by a new generation of men.' Marx rejected the conspiratorial and elitist solutions offered by, for example, Arnold Rouge arguing against him:
'[the people] have no thought for the morrow and must strike all ideas from their mind…the riddle of the future will be solved by a miracle.'

For an account of the break on December 31st, 1850 at a party hosted by Julian Harney [ Marx called him 'Hiphiporah Harney' for his zealous organizing of fund-raising parties.] see Collected Works Vol 10, (2004) pp 626-8. Harney's wife Mary insulted Helen Macfarlane and Marx blamed him for not allowing her to reply 'and so break with the only collaborator on his sprouting rag who had any original ideas – a rare bird, on his paper.' The source for Macfarlane is now Schoyen The Chartist Challenge (1958). She married a man Francis Proust who Black (2004) pp xxix-xxx speculates was mentally ill. They emigrated to South Africa in 1852 he was dropped off in France and the daughter died upon arrival. Two years later Helen was living with an unmarried sister near [200 metres] from where Engels lived with the Burns sisters. She married in 1856 back into her own class in terms of status and education to a widower Rev John Wilkinson Edwards who had graduated from Oxford. Edwards had some 'controversy with 'traditionalists' at his first parish but moved to Nantwich, St-Michael's Baddeley. She died the same age as Flora Tristan, 41 but an Anglican Christian.

Eric Hobsbawm gets the 1850 translation by Helen Macfarlane totally wrong in his 2012 introduction to the Verso edition. I think he must have been maintaining the old Stalinist tactic of making the facts fit the line which was Samuel Moore's 1888 translation had become the Standard English Edition after being given the approval of Engels (Marx had died in 1883) and was therefore considered superior. Hobsbawm fabricated an incident where Macfarlane' insulted 'either Marx or Engels'. This was not the case. Julian Harney had organised a fundraiser for the

Fraternal Democrats during which Harney's wife insulted Macfarlane who was not allowed to even the score verbally by Julian Harney. Marx later castigated him over the incident which saw the Red Republican lose the only writer he believed was capable of 'independent thought.'.

## Significant letter to J Bloch, London, 21st September 1890 Frederick Engels.

'According to the materialist conception of history, the ultimately determining element in history is the production and reproduction of real life. Other than this neither Marx nor I have ever asserted. Hence if somebody twists this into saying that the economic element is the only determining one, he transforms that proposition into a meaningless, abstract, senseless phrase. The economic situation is the basis, but the various elements of the superstructure—political forms of the class struggle and its results, to wit: constitutions established by the victorious class after a successful battle, etc., juridical forms, and even the reflexes of all these actual struggles in the brains of the participants, political, juristic, philosophical theories, religious views and their further development into systems of dogmas—also exercise their influence upon the course of the historical struggles and in many cases preponderate in determining their form.'

Nigel Pearce

## The Condition of England Novel.

Writers such as Charles Dickens, Elizabeth Gaskell, Charlotte Brontë and Charles Kingsley Alton Locke based on Thomas Cooper who was a leading Chartist and poet illuminated contemporary social problems through detailed descriptions of poverty and inequality.
Elizabeth Gaskell, Mary Burton was Gaskell's first Condition of England Novel, written in 1848 the same year as the Communist Manifesto. It is almost melodramatic and concludes with a working-class assassin and his sister 'the butterfly' being buried in unconsecrated ground. North and South. A Condition of England question novel written in 1854 is more sophisticated but generically moves between political realism and the sentimental. The genre was derived from an 1839 essay by Thomas Carlyle: 'The Condition of England' in which he lamented the social conditions of the day fearing proletarian revolution. They had indeed been several armed uprisings the year before Carlyle's essay connected to Chartism.

A problem for these writers was the concluding chapters. How to conclude an exposure of social wrongs with just variants on reform.
Lukács The Meaning of Contemporary Realism is significant as he regarded 'critical realism' i.e., bourgeois writing which understands the 'typicality' rather than the 'topicality' can be equal to or even superior to 'socialist realism' when it deteriorated into verisimilitude or Naturalism.

## Chapter Two.

## Death and Resurrection in Nantwich, 1861.

The years 1838-48 saw an upsurge in proletarian activity in Britain and a corresponding increase in interest in both poetry and literature. The defeat of 'the Charter and something more' in England, the revolutions of 1848 in Europe and the cooling of the insurrectionary aspirations of the Irish people all led to defeat for the progressive movement. It was in this context that Helen Macfarlane came to prominence as a revolutionary activist, philosopher as the first published translator of Hegel into English in June 1850 [David Black and Ben Watson [Radical Philosophy 187(Sept/Oct 2014)] show conclusively. But it was a contradictory movement, it illustrated 'uneven and combined development' to coin the name of a theory developed by Leon Trotsky which was at the root of many of his diatribes with Stalin and his followers. Talk of uneven development becomes dominant in Trotsky's writings from 1927 onwards when he homed it into a sophisticated instrument to explain the demise of and contradictions within the Chinese revolution of the mid-1920's (see Trotsky, Leon, Leon Trotsky on China, Pathfinder,1976.) From this date, whenever the law is mentioned, the claim consistently made for it is that 'the entire history of mankind is governed by the law of uneven development'." (Ian D. Thatcher, "Uneven and combined development", Revolutionary Russia, Vol. 4 No. 2, 1991, p. 237.) Although Trotsky first developed the theory in Results and Prospects (1905) and its explanatory value is of potential use here. Essentially it illustrates how the two motions of the dialectic, quantitative and qualitative can be applied to the uneven development within and between different countries. Also, to cultural phenomena which are not simply reflexive of an epoch but interdependent over the process of history as in his defence of Dante as being a genius in U.S.S.R.,1924. We can see how it was an anathema to Stalin's mechanistic thinking of, for instance, 'socialism in one country'.

Helen Macfarlane almost anticipated Trotsky in Red Republican, 22nd June 1850.:
The golden age, sung by the poets and prophets of all times and nations, from Hesiod and Isaiah to Cervantes and Shelley, the Paradise was never lost…this spirit, I say, has descended now upon the multitudes, and has consecrated them to the service of the new – and yet old – religion of Social Democracy.

However, her latent religiosity is there. Not in the reference to the Bible Isaiah and Milton Paradise Lost. Rather in the registers of 'descended now upon the multitudes' and 'new and yet – old religion of Social Democracy.' At this period in England, Social Democracy referenced one epithet: Revolution. Yet Helen Macfarlane had not thrown off the mantle of Utopian Socialism. She was somewhat akin to Flora Tristan, the French Utopian Socialist, who drove herself into an early grave through exhaustion in her attempts to rouse the French masses to build Workers Palaces. Tristan predated Marx and Engels and they defended her ideas in The Holy Family. Helen

Macfarlane's incipient Christianity was, I argue, present because of her Idealist reading of Kant and Hegel where unlike Marx she had not 'turned Hegel on his head'. We can understand this clearly here in Red Republican 20th July 1850: Red Republicanism, or democracy, is a protest against the using up of man by man. It is the endeavour to reduce the golden rule of Jesus to practice. Modern democracy is Christianity in a form adapted to the wants of the present age. It is Christianity divested of its mythological envelope. It is the idea appearing as pure thought, independent of history and tradition.


Chapter Three.

Eleanor Marx: A Dreamer of Absolutes.

Of course, people were aware of Eleanor 'Tussey' Marx who was Karl Marx's youngest and most talented daughter. However, it was only with 'second-wave' feminism that she attracted serious academic interest and meaningful studies of Eleanor Marx came to fruition. Firstly, the mould-breaking: Chuschich Tsuzuki The Life of Eleanor Marx,1855-1898: A socialist tragedy, (1967), secondly, an obscure work Ronald Florence (1975). Marx's Daughters: Eleanor Marx, Rosa Luxemburg, Angelica Balabanoff. These were followed by what is considered by many to be the authoritative text Yvonne Kapp Eleanor Marx: A Biography (2018) which was initially published as two volumes in the 1970s and took the standard 'line' of the CPGB of its time, revisionism. However, E.P. Thompson wrote a pertinent response in 1976:

But it is not an objective study. The reader who does not like to be manipulated – to be nudged through the evidence towards a prescribed conclusion, now asked to turn his head this way and now ordered to close his eyes, and now shown only an approved portion of the evidence – such a reader will still prefer Chushichi Tsuzuki's ten-year-old biography. Tsuzuki lays out very clearly, and sometimes tersely, the evidence, and invites the reader to form a judgement. Kapp does not. She is wholly entitled to write a very different, and (as she supposes) less 'academic' biography. This will be, for many readers, the virtue of her book. It is, without any pretence, engagingly partisan. She seeks to enter without reserve into the consciousness of her heroine – or hero.

Indeed, Kapp's massive narrative concludes with the suicide of Eleanor Marx and does not go beyond it possibly because of the constraints of being a lifelong member of the CPGB. While Tsuzuki's investigates the circumstances after the suicide with contemporary documents. She finds in a letter from Bernstein to Adler that after the German Party representatives who travelled to England that upon hearing that Edward Aveling had decided to attend a football match the afternoon after Eleanor's death:

If there was no party interest to take into consideration the people would have torn Aveling to pieces.

Then a period of neglect until the next crisis of Capitalism and Rachel Holmes, from a Left-Feminist perspective, argued that Eleanor Marx attempted to build a United Front of women and workers Eleanor Marx: A Life (2014). This is a useful book because it illuminates much of her subject's interest in literature and culture and convincingly argues that her interest in the Arts was not detached from the proletarian movement. She took literature and drama to the masses. Its flaw is that it drifts towards Left Bourgeois Feminism and attempts to argue that Eleanor Marx held those views which is questionable. She might have believed in a form of dual-systems theory in 1886 when she published The Woman Question: from a socialist point of view. However, Lise Vagal argued that was the leading position on the Left following (Engels 1968) August Bebel (1910) and that there was later a different 'line' that emanated from Lenin. 'Lenin criticised the backwardness of many male comrades on this issue..." unfortunately, we may say of many of our comrades 'scratch the surface and a philistine appears.' A Neo-Trotskyist 'line' is pursued by Siobhan Brown . Although it is my sense that these studies tended to err on the personal as political rather than create a theoretical structure for the analysis of Eleanor Marx's contribution to the international socialist movement and her death, valuable though they are.

## Chapter Four.

## Ibsen's Doll's House. A Study in Patriarchy.

Eleanor Marx's suicide cannot be explained by simply the metanarratives of Radical Feminism or indeed, Orthodox Marxism. Equally, it stretches congruity to pass it off as Edward Aveling merely being a 'bad apple' who could have driven Karl Marx's most politically engaged daughter to suicide. Nevertheless, Kapp notes:

> The truth is that in moral terms Aveling presented something akin to an optical illusion: looked at in one light, he could be seen as feckless, happy-go-lucky but fundamentally sound; in another, as an unmitigated scoundrel.

However, I will argue that the circumstances represented a complex conundrum requiring a new reading. It is significant that her mother said she was 'political from top to bottom' Also, Eleanor would quote in a letter to a sister that her father said 'Tussy is me' (Karl Marx quoted by Eleanor Marx to Laura Lafargue, 23 April 1886 (Holmes, 2014, p.251.). While Engels said she: 'was the living and practical realisation of Marx's ideas on the ground' (Alexander (2007). Intriguingly Eleanor

Marx said of herself:
> The artistic life is the only life a free woman can live.

It is possible to posit a parallel with Virginia Woolf A Room of One's Own here.

Sally Alexander (2007) argues that there was a cult of suicide around middle-class Victorian women social reformers. I shall seek an explanation of greater theoretical capacity in the work of Louis Althusser. Although it is necessary to understand that Althusser was writing in a French intellectual milieu argues Callinicos (2012 pp 267-74). Thus, we cannot ignore Saussure's linguistics, an autonomous system of sign/signifier/signified which was applied to anthropology by Levi-Strauss where he privileges the signifier over the signified, with the latter becoming 'unconscious' and Lucan's Freudianism. One key concept is 'the problematic' that Althusser described thus: 'the objective internal reference system of its particular themes, the system of questions commanding the answers given.' (Althusser, For Marx, 1979, p.67n). By this, he meant an objective structure which allows what can be 'said' or not. As Callinicos describes:

The problematic of a theory is objective: it cannot be reduced to the beliefs of the author of the theory; it is extractable only by means of a symptomatic reading.'

So, as Luke Ferretter (2006, p.35-36) points out some of Sylvia Plath's more violent imagery before her suicide in 1963 could be explained through a symptomatic reading in that she did not have a second wave feminist 'problematic' to answer her writing, it did not exist. As Althusser maintained:

Every ideology must be regarded as a real whole, internally unified by its own problematic, so that it is impossible to extract one element without altering its meaning.

I shall suggest Eleanor Marx's suicide was similar to Sylvia Plath's because she did not have a revolutionary 'problematic' or an alternative system to answer her questions. Thus, a 'symptomatic' reading illustrates the Paris Commune had failed and a new problematic was not formed until October 1917. Hence, in Althusserian terms:

> (A symptomatic reading) divulges the undivulged event in the text it reads, and in the same movement relates it to a different text, present as a necessary absence of the first.

Also, for Althusser, we are unconsciously interpellated by ideology. It 'hails' us, becomes us we believe it to be ours. Thus, "Ideology and Ideological State Apparatuses (Notes Towards an Investigation [1970)" Althusser introduced the concepts of Ideological State Apparatuses (ISAs), Repressive State Apparatuses (RSAs), a revisiting of Marx on ideology, and interpellation. In his writing for example, when a police officer shouts (or hails) "Hey, you there!" and an individual turn around and so-to-speak 'answers' the call, he becomes a subject. Althusser argues that this is because the individual has realised that the hailing was addressed at him which makes him the subject. As Althusser argues this is essential for the ideology of bourgeois democracy or, indeed, I shall suggest patriarchy. Further, Althusser maintained, it was required to have a complexified understanding of how the superstructure creates

the ideologically necessary prerequisites for the infrastructure to reproduce the conditions of capitalism. It was not possible for the bourgeoisie to rule simply by forced R.S.A.s i.e. the police and army etc. Rather it is necessary if social reproduction is to take place for the proletariat to consent. Hegemony would be achieved, in Althusser's view, by I.S.A.s the churches, media, cultural practices. I would argue that one of the cultural practices that are reproduced is Patriarchy and agree with Althusser that these are reinforced unconsciously by interpellation or 'hailing' as described above. Althusser drew on the work on misrecognition at the 'mirror stage" [stade du miroir] noted by Jacque Lucan in the development of very young children whereby, he argued, the ego was formed. Thus, when combined with Althusser's Neo-Marxism we can understand how the subject may misrecognize socially produced relations as their actual self. Hence my contention here is that although Eleanor Marx had access to both Engels, Origins of the Family, Private Property, and the State and less significantly August Bebel Women and Socialism they existed in the superstructure as ideological abstractions. These are in a dialectical relationship to the economic base as Marx and Engels had realised: The ideas of the ruling class are in every epoch the ruling ideas,
i.e. the class, which is the ruling material force of society, is at the same time its ruling intellectual force [...] The ruling ideas are nothing more than the ideal expression of the dominant material relationships.

In a recollection of a friend, Eleanor Marx showed herself to have been interpellated by Patriarchy ironically in opposition to Ibsen's Nora whom she had admired:

> "One alternative," she is reported to have said, "is to leave. Edward and live by myself. I can't do that; it would drive him to ruin and wouldn't really help …. It was Edward who really brought out the feminine in me. I was irresistibly drawn to him … Our tastes were much the same … We agreed on Socialism. We both loved the theatre… We could work together effectively.

## Chapter Five.

### Hot Autumn: Alexandra Kollontai, the Doll's House Unlocked.

I nevertheless endeavour to move beyond some of Althusser's entrapping ideological manacles and would argue that in time of severe political and social crisis under capitalism that Lukács is cogent in providing a greater degree of agency and thus transformation:

As the decisive battle in the class struggle approaches, the power of a true or false theory to accelerate or retard progress grows in proportion. The 'realm of freedom', the end of the 'pre-history of mankind' means precisely that the power of the objectified, reified relations between men begins to revert to man. The closer this process comes to its goal the more urgent it becomes for the proletariat to understand its own historical mission and the more vigorously and directly proletarian class consciousness will determine each of its actions.

Lukács also endeavours to explain why this has not happened by an argument emanating from Marx's commodity fetishism taken to its logical outcome in an advanced capitalist society where the commodity is pervasive, and reification prevents the majority of workers from understanding capitalism as a Totality. However, he argues, the proletariat will become, because of historical 'necessity', "the identical subject-object of history" (Lukács (2010) p 258-59).

However, it is necessary to elucidate both the contents and circumstances of Lukacs History and Class Consciousness. He had previously written The Theory of the Novel (1916) in which he had noted the decline of writing from the organic unity of Greek Epic to the fragmentation of the modern novel. Lukacs argued this was caused by the atomisation within capitalism i.e. Ancient Greek society was a Totality while the monopoly-finance Capital of the period was not. Lukacs at this period designated his position as one of a 'Romantic Anti-Capitalist'. 'However, the October Revolution in Russia of 1917 provided him with a solution to his problem. How to remedy the fragmentation of capitalism. In a monumental study written over a period of four years Lukacs not only provided the theoretical architecture to support his claim that the proletariat and ultimately proletarian revolution where the remedy for an alienating and dehumanising capitalism. He also, somewhat remarkably, anticipated the publication of the young Marx's Economic and Philosophical Manuscripts which appeared in 1932 with his concepts of Totality and reification. Yet Lukacs was not only prophetic of Marx's claims he also advanced Marxist theory. It should be considered that Lukacs unlike Engels in Anti-During and Dialectics of Nature understood Marxism as a theory which, at that time, had not the capacity to apply the Dialectic to the Natural Sciences. Rather, for Lukacs, Marxism in H.C.C. provides an explanation of the Antinomies of Bourgeois Thought and a theory of Proletarian Consciousness as a Totalising force. Lukács endeavours to answer the question 'what is Orthodox Marxism? After the failure of the Second International to organise against the imperialism of WWI and the success of the Third International, (all be it short-lived) in establishing a new model of society based on worker's power and the freedom of the individual when positioned within her social being.

Lukacs wanted to understand why bourgeois philosophy, principally Classical German Philosophy, Immanuel Kant and Hegel had not solved the major problem of philosophy of their epoch, the relationship of the subject to the object, a problem of epistemology. This had manifested itself previously to Kant in the two schools of thought: Rationalists who believed thought was paramount and was a preliminary to the knowledge of the world if it was possible to know the world. Thus, thought was a priori or before to human experience. Manifestations of this school would be pure mathematics and ontological proofs of the existence of God. Alternatively, there were a British school of philosophers especially Locke and Hume who believed human knowledge was a posteriori or after experience. Humans are tabula rasa, a blank slate on which experience makes it marks. This is associated with justification that depends on experience or empirical evidence, as with most aspects of science. However, this divide in Western philosophy can be traced to Plato and Aristotle

Immanuel Kant, who was a theist, after reading the sceptic Hume, was minded to solve the subject-object problem. Firstly, he argued, there is a phenomenological world we can see but we cannot know because it is merely that of 'appearances' However, beyond this lies the world of essences we cannot know through the senses he called the noumenal world or 'things-in-themselves'. We cannot know that world like the phenomenological world which consists of 'things-as-they-appear-to-us.' He tried to fuse the two with an a synthetic a priori. In order to comprehend that concept, consider these two sets of relations:

a) matters of fact: observed truths, such as 'bread nourishes'.
b) relations of ideas: logical truths, such as 'two plus two equals four.'

Our initial cognisance is that 'relations of ideas' are always a priori and 'matters of fact' are always a posteriori which was the position held before Kant. Rather what Kant did was that he combined the a priori with matters of fact and created a new category in philosophy the synthetic a priori. Thus, we can gain some knowledge of the world, 'matters of fact', just by thinking. Had he persuasively solved the subject-object problem? No, argued Lukacs because they were not a synthesis. Not an 'identical subject-object.' Lukács maintained the possibility to know this could only be solved dialectically and thus with a knowledge of Hegelian philosophy and dialectics.

It is of significance to this thesis that Helen Macfarlane was conversant with both the ideas of Immanuel Kant and Hegel:
To understand Hegel…it is important to be aware that
 Hegel was writing shortly after the death of Kant. Indeed, Hegel's concepts of alienation and dialectics were central to both Marx's and, arguably to a lesser extent, Engels understanding of the world. Hegel's Phenomenology of the Spirit examines the unresolved problem of the relationship between the object of the Spirit and of the subject of the Spirit. Unlike Kant, Hegel comprehended the 'Absolute Spirit' as distinct from the transcendental concept of God as a deity. The 'Absolute Spirit', i.e. God, is not separated from the world that it had created. Although, he also argues, the world 'seems to inflict on self-consciousness from without.' The 'Absolute Spirit' rather self-creates both itself and the world until, they achieve a synthesis in what he would later suggest is the Prussian state. Here we can see the divide between the Young or Left Hegelians who concentrated on the process of transformation and Right Hegelians who sought to maintain the status qua. Hegel argued the world is 'the work of the self-consciousness', it is 'the self-consciousness acting on the world' but the world is somehow alien to it.   Hence, Hegel developed

some terms to attempt to answer Kant's dilemma. Firstly, regarding consciousness as he was not a Materialist rather being an Idealist, 'being-in-itself' which is the object of consciousness of the Spirit and 'being-for itself' which is the subject of consciousness of the Spirit. Therefore, we can ascertain a degree of alienation between object and subject. Hegel's remedy was 'being-in-and-for-itself', the incarnation of the Spirit in the World by Will, specifically in the Germanic State. However, the concept of alienation was developed persuasively by Marx in Economic and Philosophical Manuscripts (1844) where he discussed the object of the worker's labour being alienated from him or her, the subject.

How is the movement of the Absolute Spirit self-creation to be explained? Hegel was absolutely clear:

[...] contradiction is at the root of all movement and life, and it is only so far as it contains a Contradiction that anything moves and has impulse or activity.

Here we can understand Hegel's particular philosophical method which was
 dialectical. Therefore, it is possible to ascertain the Hegelian foundation for both Lukacs's concepts of Totality and reification. Nevertheless, he would follow Marx in providing a materialist orientation.

Therefore, because the proletariat must ultimately or 'in the last instance' create a Totality which can only be a manifestation of Communism. This is because, for Lukacs, the proletariat has an 'ascribed consciousness'. This he had derived from Weber's concept of ideal 'types. Therefore, although the proletariat as a group of individuals may not seem the class whose 'world-historic mission' it is to create Communism they will as Marx and Engels argued in The German Ideology purge themselves 'of the' in the process:

The revolution is necessary, therefore, not only because the ruling class cannot be overthrown in any other way, but also because t muck of ages he class overthrowing it can only in a revolution succeed in ridding itself of all the muck of ages and become fitted to found society anew .

Another way of articulating this was by Marx's employment of Hegelian terminology i.e. with a material foundation in the class struggle. Although Marx does not use the phrase 'class-in-itself' directly he does imply it in The Poverty of Philosophy where he utilises the term 'class-for-itself'.

Economic conditions had first transformed the mass of the country into workers. The combination of capital has created for this mass a common situation, common interests. This mass is thus already a class as against capital but not yet for itself. In the struggle, of which we have noted only a few phases, this mass becomes united, and constitutes itself as a class for itself. The interests it defends become class interests. But the struggle of class against class is a political struggle.

The whole of Lukacs methodology is not a variation on Hegelian Idealism as some claim. Therefore, we can see how Lukacs amends and develops Marx's method and then his conception of commodity fetishism:

as against this, the commodity-form, and the value-relation of the products of labour within which it appears, have absolutely no connection with the physical nature of the commodity and the material relations arising out of this. It is nothing but the definite social relation between men themselves which assumes here, for them, the fantastic form of a relation between things. In order, therefore, to find an analogy we must take flight into the misty realm of religion. There the products of the human brain appear as autonomous figures endowed with a life of their own, which enter into relations both with each other and with the human race. So, it is in the world of commodities with the products of men's hands. I call this the fetishism which attaches itself to the products of labour as soon as they are produced as commodities and is therefore inseparable from the production of commodities. Hence, it is clear that Lukacs developed Marx's theory of commodity fetishism into
 an advanced model of reification:
'the function of these unmediated concepts that have been derived from the fetishist forms of objectivity is to make the phenomena of capitalist society appear as supra-historical essences.

The knowledge of the real, objective nature of a phenomenon, the knowledge of its historical character and the knowledge of its actual function in the totality of society form, therefore, a single, undivided act of cognition.

Lukacs developed a sophisticated theory of Historical Materialism and can be compared to

Leon Trotsky when he understood that the proletariat is not a mechanistic cog turned by a larger wheel of History. Rather he argued: 'The class consciousness of the proletariat does not develop uniformly throughout the proletariat, parallel to the economic crisis.' Lukacs interest in literary criticism and poetics is pertinent because they form a Totality with the philosophy expressed in History and Class Consciousness and Lenin: a study in the unity of his thought. Essentially the same narrative of a 'de-reified' & Totalised proletariat is applied to literature. He employs the ideas of critical realism as a method of distancing himself from the excesses of the 1934 Writers Congress in the U.S.S.R. with its call for a 'Romantic Socialist Realism'. Critical Realism understands both the temporal reality and contradictions of the epoch it is describing but, according to Lukacs it lacks the world-historic overview of Marxism. Lukacs argued the simply using the form and content of Socialist Realism is inadequate. He criticises the Stalinist orthodoxy of the period by appealing to both Marx and Lenin as a defence:

> It is no accident that Lenin, like Marx, should regard Tolstoy's realism – in spite of its ideological shortcomings - as a model of the literature of the future.

Whereas he argues the modernist writer is caught up in his own inner contradictions. Ultimately, for Lukacs a Socialist literature will gestate when the socio-historical conditions are ripe. He did as a mature critic have unrealistically high expectations of Aleksandr Solzhenitsyn.

Alexandra Kollontai was a brilliant early Marxist Feminist as is illustrated here in The Social Basis of the Woman Question:

The women's world is divided, just as is the world of men, into two camps: the interests and aspirations of one group bring it close to the bourgeois class, while the other group has close connections to the proletariat, and its claims for liberation encompass a full solution to the woman question. Thus, although both camps follow the general slogan of the "liberation of women," their aims and interests are different. Each of the groups unconsciously takes its starting point from the interests and aspirations of its own class, which gives a specific class colouring to the targets and tasks it sets for itself... however apparently radical the demands of the feminists, one must not lose sight of the fact that the feminists cannot, on account of their class position, fight for that fundamental transformation of society, without which the liberation of women cannot be complete.

Thus, I am inclined to follow Judith Orr Marxism and Women's Liberation and Sharon Smith Women and Socialism who argue Women's Oppression can only be resolved in a Communist society. We can perceive Nikolai Chernyshevsky What Is to Be Done (1863) hero Vera Pavlovna as the successful embodiment of New Woman. Therefore, I am persuaded by Alexandra Kollontai's argument:

In place of the old individualist and egotistic family, there will rise a universal family of workers, in which all the workers, men and
 women will be, above all workers, comrades.

Hence this would facilitate the appropriate status of Helen Macfarlane and Eleanor Marx amongst the pantheon of the great international Marxist thinkers and revolutionaries.

## **Conjectures and Reawakening.**

Simone de Beauvoir, The Second Sex.
'One is not born a woman, rather one becomes a woman.'
Kate Millet, Sexual Politics. Anti-Freud = Phallocentric criticism.
"'It is interesting that many women do not recognise themselves as discriminated against; no better proof could be found of the totality of their conditioning."
— Kate Millett, Sexual Politics

Elaine Showalter, A Literature of Their Own: Gynocentric writing Women's writing by and for women according to Elaine Showalter, argued gynocritics is the study of not only the female as a gender status but also the 'internalized consciousness' of the female. The uncovering of the female subculture and exposition of a female model is the intention of gynocriticism, comprising recognition of a distinct female where a female identity is sought free from the definitions and oppositions. Elaine Showalter noted:
'In this generation female suicides become conspicuous for the first time; Eleanor Marx, Charlotte Mew, Adela Nicolson and Amy Levy.

Lise Vogel, Marxism, and the Oppression of Women: Towards a Unitary Theory.

Notes towards an understanding of her work.

1) Dual system theories, which see "two equally powerful motors driving] the development of history: the class struggle and the sex struggle", Vogel set out to construct a unitary theory that transcended the separation of production and reproduction.

2) Socialist feminists tended to argue that women's oppression operates relatively autonomously from capitalist exploitation. Women's oppression was, for them, located in the sphere of reproduction, exploitation in the sphere of production. In such a dual systems perspective, the struggle against exploitation was regarded as related to but distinct from the struggle for women's liberation.

3) Some socialist feminists went beyond simply identifying these two relatively autonomous spheres of exploitation and oppression, attempting to theorise the relationship between them through analysing the role of women in domestic labour. Margaret Benston in 1969, followed by Peggy Morton in 1971, laid out the basic principles of a materialist analysis of domestic housework. Both understood domestic labour as composed of material activities that result in products consumed within the household. The positive contribution of the domestic labour debate was the insight that the work that women did in the home sustained the household unit and enabled some of its members to go to work each day.

4) Vogel argues that, while the earliest observations made by Benston and Morton that domestic labour produced use values that are

consumed within the household proved essentially correct, domestic labour does not produce exchange values, therefore neither does it produce value, nor can it be considered productive or unproductive.

5) Ultimately, despite their intentions, the socialist feminists failed organically to link gender and class, production and reproduction, exploitation, and oppression. Vogel attempted to theorise women's oppression while avoiding the pitfalls and limitations inherent in the domestic labour debate. In particular, she formulated her theory by taking up and extending the categories elaborated by Marx in Capital.

6) But, controversially, Vogel also argued that the limitations of socialist feminist theory derived from what has often been seen as a key Marxist work on the question of women's oppression: Frederick Engels's The Origin of the Family, Private Property and the State.

7) For a response to Vogel, See Tony Cliff, Class Struggle and Women's Liberation (London, Bookmarks) 1984, pp 67-109. Vogel criticises Zetkin's focus on women solely as workers, arguing that this makes the wives and daughters of the working class who do not participate in wage labour invisible, she does not engage with the key argument Zetklin was making, namely that female workers gained collective power as part of the working class as they assumed a role in capitalist production. . Also, Zetkin's argues that working class women and men should unite as their interest is in creating socialism.

8) While many of Vogel's specific criticisms of Engels's text are justified, her overall

characterisation of Origins as a "defective text" is unnecessarily dismissive.

9) Engels argued that women's oppression came about at a particular historical juncture; the shift from subsistence to surplus-producing societies. While subsistence societies might be characterised by a division of labour between men, who focused on hunting and fishing, and women, who oversaw gathering and the household, the former did not carry greater importance than the latter. The equal importance accorded to hunting and gathering laid the basis for both men and women's participation in collective decision making. Engels argued that oppressive relationships between men and women were absent in these societies; male supremacy only arose with the rise of class society. In primitive societies men owned the instruments necessary to hunt, fish, cultivate, etc, and therefore when production methods changed and societies began to produce a social surplus, it was men who controlled that surplus. In order for men to pass on wealth to descendants, women needed to be tightly controlled. The origin of the monogamous family lay with the development of private property, and, with the advent of monogamous marriage, the nuclear family became the basic economic unit of society. Engels described this as "the world historic defeat of the female sex"; women had become "a mere instrument for the production of children" and were reduced to servitude to men.

10) Vogel argues of Origins, that firstly it misses the significance of the working-class household as an essential social unit, not for the

holding of property but for the reproduction of the working class itself. Second, it overlooks the ways in which a material basis for male supremacy is constituted within the proletarian household. And third, it vastly underestimates the variety of ideological and psychological factors that provide a continuing foundation for male supremacy in the working-class family. These are well made arguments.

11)     Engels failed fully to theorise the character of women's oppression under capitalism in Origins—but this was not Engels's main intention in this work. Engels provides a historical account of the rise of the family as class society develops, rather than specifically setting out to theorise women's oppression under capitalism, arguing that gender roles are social and historical rather than fixed transhistorical entities. Vogel in fact fails to grapple with the historical issue of the origins of women's oppression. Thus, while she correctly argues that the family "is not a timeless universal of human society", she fails to explain why or to explain when the family arose or how its form has changed alongside changes in the mode of production.

12)     Vogel's main question with Origins is its supposed propagation of the dual systems perspective. Vogel accuses Engels of distinguishing between two types of production: first, the production of means of subsistence, and second, the production of human beings. This theoretical dualism, she argues, ultimately bears responsibility for the dual systems perspectives of socialist feminism. In the offending passage Engels writes:

'According to the materialistic conception, the determining factor in history is, in the final instance, the production and reproduction of immediate life. This, again, is of twofold character: on the one side, the production of the means of existence, of food, clothing and shelter and the tools necessary for that production; on the other side, the production of human beings themselves, the propagation of the species. The social organisation under which the people of a particular historical epoch and a particular country live is determined by both kinds of production: by the stage of development of labour on the one hand and of the family on the other'.

13) Engels's remarks appear to offer authoritative Marxist backing for the socialist feminist movement's focus on the family, sex-divisions of labour, and unpaid domestic work, as well as for its theoretical dualism and its strategic commitment to the autonomous organisation of women.

14) However, firstly, in the US the women's movement was largely composed of cross-class alliances. It had a decidedly different character from the British women's movement, which had a greater orientation on the working class and trade unions or at least to a larger extent., Secondly, Vogel's belief in actual existing socialism having been present in the U.S.S.R., China and Cuba rather than them being 'degenerated workers states'(Trotsky) or 'bureaucratic state capitalism' (Tony Cliff). Vogel's version of "socialism" has not precipitated the erosion, and eventual abolition, of women's oppression in such societies and, consequently, a distinct movement for women's

liberation becomes necessary. Therefore, while repeatedly criticising the tendency of socialist feminists to treat the fight for socialism and women's liberation as autonomous spheres, Vogel ends up advocating a strategy that tacitly replicates this dualism

15) [Marx's] notes suggest that, for Marx, the development of class society and women's oppression are part of the same historical process, but in a somewhat different way than that described later by Engels... For Marx, there had been no "world historic defeat of the female sex." The condition of women in society is and has varied. This is just as true of the time before the introduction of patriarchy as in the period of patriarchy. Instead of seeing this development in a linear way, Marx appears to have been working out a dialectical history of these processes.

Nevertheless, Sharon Smith is absolutely clear and persuasive here:

The revolutionary potential of the working class as it is currently composed has yet to be seen, but it can most certainly be anticipated. When that time comes, working-class women will no doubt take centre stage.

Judith Orr (2015 p,199 & p 220) cogently positioned the ideas of Eleanor Marx in the revolutionary socialist problematic of the October 1917 Russian Revolution. That would have resolved the question of unconscious interpellation by patriarchy in her relationship with Edward Aveling addressed above because as Lenin was to argue:

The experience of all liberation movements has shown that the success of a revolution depends on how much the women take part in it.


## Conclusion.

Hence, I have attempted to create a dialectical synthesis of theory and 'lived experience.' A literary praxis in this thesis which illustrates both 'hidden histories' of women in the British Left during the 19th century and provides the theoretical apparatus with which to do so. I have, also, drawn parallels with Patriarchal oppression in Eleanor Marx and Sylvia Plath and their deaths. However, conclusively, I locate the demise of both Helen Macfarlane and Eleanor Marx in the failure of the Marxist current within the British proletariat to generalise into the wider working-class movement and thus create the potential for the emancipation of all the oppressed. Because, as Eleanor Marx argued when the engines of proletarian gender and class interests are united:

We are not women arrayed in struggle against men but we are in struggle against the exploiters.

Thus, when the proletariat is united as a 'class-for itself', it would discover its inherent or 'ascribed consciousness' and lead the festival of the oppressed in creating 'the-identical-subject-object' of history' (Lukács), socialism. A dialectical synthesis has been attempted between 'the lived experience' of these women and the 'metanarratives' of Marxism and Feminism. These models have been shown to provide an analytical counterpoint to the dissonance of oppression, estrangement, and exploitation. We may recollect Walter Benjamin: 'There is no document of civilisation which is not at the same time a document of barbarism...A historical materialist regards it as his task to brush history against the grain.' . This remains our task in the current circumstances, I would argue.

## Appendix A..

### Leon Trotsky on Dante.

'If I say that the importance of the Divine Comedy lies in the fact that it gives me an understanding of the state of mind of certain classes in a certain epoch, this means that I transform it into a mere historical document, for, as a work of art, the Divine Comedy must speak in some way to my feelings and moods. Dante's work may act on me in a depressing way, fostering pessimism and despondency in me, or, on the contrary, it may rouse, inspire, encourage me. This is the fundamental relationship between a reader and a work of art. Nobody, of course, forbids a reader to assume the role of a researcher and approach the Divine Comedy as merely an historical document. It is clear, though, that these two approaches are on two different levels, which, though connected, do not overlap. How is it thinkable that there should be not an historical but a directly aesthetic relationship between us and a medieval Italian book? This is explained by the fact that in class society, in spite of all its changeability, there are certain common features. Works of art developed in a medieval Italian city can, we find, affect us too. What does this require? A small thing: it requires that these feelings and moods shall have received such broad, intense, powerful expression as to have raised them above the limitations of the life of those days. Dante was, of course, the product of a certain social milieu. But Dante was a genius. He raised the experience of his epoch to a tremendous artistic height. And if we, while today approaching other works of medieval literature merely as objects of study, approach the Divine Comedy as a source of artistic perception, this happens not because Dante was a Florentine petty bourgeois of the 13th century but, to a considerable extent, in spite of that circumstance. Let us take, for instance, such an elementary psychological feeling as fear of death. This feeling is characteristic not only of man but also of animals. In man it first found simple articulate expression, and later also artistic expression. In different ages, in different social milieu, this expression has changed, that is to say, men have feared death in different ways. And nevertheless, what was said on this score not only by Shakespeare, Byron, Goethe, but also by the Psalmist, can move us.

Leon Trotsky Class and Art: (May 1924). Delivered: May 9, 1924. Speech during discussion at the Press Department of the Central Committee of the RCP(B) on Party Policy in the Field of Imaginative Literature. Publisher: New Park, London, September 1974, Reprinted from Fourth International of July 1967.

## Appendix B.
## Raymond Williams on Gramsci.

The British cultural theorist Raymond Williams notes of Gramsci that this was a huge advance on those critical positions that assumed that ideologies were simply false ideas imposed upon people. Gramsci's analysis, he writes: supposes the existence of something which is truly total ... but which is lived at such a depth, which saturates society to such an extent, and which even constitutes the substance and limit of common sense for most people under its sway, that it corresponds to the reality of [their] social experience ... If ideology were merely some abstract, imposed set of notions, if our social and political and cultural ideas and assumptions and habits were merely the result of specific manipulation, of a kind of overt training which might be simply ended or withdrawn, then the society would be very much easier to move and to change than in practice it has ever been or is.
- Raymond Williams Problems of Materialism (London, Verso 1980): p. 37.

## Bibliography

Primary Sources

Adoratsky. V, The History of the Communist Manifesto of Marx, and Engels, (New York, International Publishers, 1938).

Bebel, August Women and Socialism (New York, Socialist Literature Company.1910).

Black, David [ed] Helen Macfarlane Red Republican (London, Unkant Publishers, 2014).

Chernyshevsky, Nikolay, What is to Be Done, 1888.
https://archive.org/details/cu31924096961036

Engels, Frederick Socialism: Utopian and Scientific
https://www.marxists.org/archive/marx/works/1880/soc-utop/index.htm

Engels, F, The Origins of the Family, Private Property and The State (Moscow, Progress Publishers, 1968).

Feuerbach, Ludwig The Essence of Christianity (trans) Elliot, George (Dover Philosophical Classics 2008).

Flaubert, Gustave Madame Bovary [Eleanor Marx-Aveling translation] Second Norton Critical Edition [ed] Cohen, M, (New York, W.W. Norton & Company, 2005).

Democratic Review 1849-1850 [ed] Julian Harney, (New York, Barnes and Noble, 1968).

Harney Papers [ed] Black, F & Black, R (Assen, Royal Vangorcum Ltd, 1969).
Red Republican and The Friend of the People Vols 1 & 2 1850-1851 [ed] Julian Harney. Reprint with an introduction by John Saville (London, Merlin Press, 1966).

Ibsen, Henrik A Doll's House, and Other Plays (London, Penguin Classics, 2016).
Hegel, G.W.F. Phenomenology of the Spirit (Cambridge. Cambridge University Press, 1994).
Hobsbawm, Eric [ed] The Communist Manifesto (London, Verso, 2012).
Macfarlane, Helen Remarks on the times – Apropos of Certain Passages in No.1 of Thomas Carlyle's Latter-day Pamphlets Democratic Review, June 1850. [Black [ed] 2014).

Macfarlane, Helen, 'Chartism in 1850', Red Republican, 22nd June 1850.
Howard Morton" (Helen Macfarlane), "Fine Words (Household of otherwise) Butter No Parsnips." Red Republican, 20 July 1850.
Macfarlane, Helen The Communist Manifesto, Red Republican, [November 1850, 9th, 16th, 23rd & 30th] (London, Merlin Press, 1966).

MacLellan, David [ed]The Communist Manifesto (Oxford, Oxford World Classics, 2014).

The Daughters of Marx Selected Correspondence (ed) Olga Merrier & Faith Evans (Harmondsworth, Penguin Books, 1984).

Eleanor Marx & Edward Aveling, Letters from England 1895 (London, Lawrence & Wishart, 2020).

Eleanor Marx & Edward Aveling The Working-Class Movement in America (London, Swan Sonenshein & Co, 1891).

Eleanor Marx & Edward Aveling The Women Question from a Socialist Point of View, 1886.
https://www.marxists.org › archive › eleanor-marx › works › womanq

Marx, Karl 'The Afterword' of the Second Edition of Capital Vol I (Harmondsworth, Penguin Books, 1976).

Marx & Engels Collected Works in 50 volumes. (London, Lawrence & Wishart, 2004).

Marx & Engels On Literature and Art. A Selection of Writings, [eds] L. Baxandall and S. Mora (St. Louis, Milwaukee, 1973)

Marx & Engels, Selected Correspondence (Moscow, Progress Publishers, 1965).

Moore, Samuel in cooperation with Engels The Communist Manifesto (London, 30th January 1888).
https://www.marxists.org/archive/marx/works/1848/communist-manifesto/

Ryazanoff, D Karl Marx: Man, Thinker and Revolutionist, a Symposium. (London, Martin Lawrence Limited, 1927).

The Commonweal 1887 (The Official Journal of the Socialist League), (India, Pranava Books Classic Reprints, 2019).

The Commonweal (Journal of the Socialist League).
https://www.marxists.org/history/international/social-democracy/commonweal.htm

Socialist League (UK) Archives.
http://hdl.handle.net/10622/ARCH01344

The Socialist League Address to the Trade Unions (London. Socialist League Office, 1885, Socialist Platform Reprints No. 1, 1977).

The Socialist League Leaflets and Manifestos: An Annotated Checklist (Author) Eugene D. Lemire International Review of Social History, Vol. 22, No 1 (1977).

## Secondary Sources.

Alexander, Sally (2007) Eleanor Marx's Political Legacy self-sacrifice or self-realisation. Women's History Review.
Althusser, Louis, For Marx (London, Verso, 1979).
Althusser, Louis, Ideology and Ideological State Apparatuses (Notes Towards an Investigation [1970)

Althusser, Louis, Lenin and Philosophy and other essays (Delhi, Askari Books 2009).
lthusser and Balibar Reading Capital (London, Verso, 2009).
Beauvoir, Simone de The Second Sex. (London, Vintage Classics, 1997).
Benjamin, Walter, Illuminations, [ed] Arendt Hannah (London, Pimlico, 1999).
Black, David Helen Macfarlane A Feminist, Revolutionary Journalist, and Philosopher in Mid-Nineteenth Century England (Oxford, Lexington Books, 2004).
Black, David, Ben Watson [Radical Philosophy 187, (Sept/Oct 2014) Helen Macfarlane
https://www.radicalphilosophy.com › article › helen-macfarlan

Brown, Heather A., Marx on Gender, and the Family; A Critical Study (Chicago, Haymarket Books, 2013).
Brown, Siobhan A Rebel's Guide to Eleanor Marx (London, Bookmarks, 2015).
Callinicos, Alex, Althusser's Marxism, (London, Pluto Press, 1976).
Callinicos, Alex Social Theory: A Historical Introduction. (Cambridge, Polity Press, 2012).
Camus, Albert, The Myth of Sisyphus (London, Penguin Great Ideas, 2005).
Carver, Terrell, & Farr, James The Cambridge Companion to The Communist Manifesto. (Cambridge, Cambridge University Press, 2015).
Cowling, Mark The Communist Manifesto New Interpretations (Cambridge, Edinburgh University Press, 1998).

Draper, Hal, The Adventures of the Communist Manifesto (California Centre for Socialist History, 2004).
Ferretter, Luke Louis Althusser (London, Routledge, 2006).
Foley, Barbara, Marxist Literary Criticism Today (London, Pluto Press, 2019).
Foot, Paul The Vote (London, Bookmarks, 2006).
Ginsburgh, Nicola, (2014) http://isj.org.uk/lise-vogel-and-the-politics-of-womens-liberation
Holmes, Rachel Eleanor Marx A Life, (London, Bloomsbury, 2014.)
Kapp, Yvonne Eleanor Marx, A Biography, (London, Verso, 2018.).
Selected Writings of Alexandra Kollontai (Westport, Holt, Alix [ed] CT: Lawrence Hill & Co., 1977).
Alexandra Kollontai on Women's Liberation [ed] Rosenberg, Chanie (London, Bookmarks, 1977).
V I Lenin, The Emancipation of Women (International Publishers, 1984).
Lukács, Georg History and Class Consciousness (Pontypool, The Merlin Press, 2010).
Lukács, Georg The Meaning of Contemporary Realism, (Pontypool, The Merlin Press, 2006).
McLellan, David Marx before Marxism (Harmondsworth, Penguin Books, 1970).
Millett, Kate Sexual Politics, (Urbana and Chicago, University of Illinois Press, 2000).
Orr, Judith Marxism and Women's Liberation. (London, Bookmarks, 2015).
Prawer, S.S. Karl Marx and World Literature. (London, Verso, 2015).

Schoyen, A.R. The Chartist Challenge, (London, Heinemann, 1958).

Showalter, Elaine A Literature Of Their Own: British Women Novelists from Brontë to Lessing. (London, Virago, Revised Edition 2009).

Sullivan, Terry & Gluckstein, Donny Hegel and Revolution (London, Bookmarks, 2020).

Thatcher, Ian D. "Uneven and combined development", Revolutionary Russia, Vol. 4 No. 2, 1991.

Thompson E.P. (1976).
https://www.marxists.org › archive › thompson-ep › eleanor-marx "

Trotsky, Leon Class and Art (Speech, May 9th, 1926).

Trotsky, Leon, Leon Trotsky on China, (New York Pathfinder,1976).

Trotsky, Leon Results and Prospects
http://www.marxists.org/archive/trotsky/1931/tpr/rp-index.htm

Trotsky, Leon, What Next (1932)
https://www.marxists.org/archive/trotsky/germany/1932-ger/index.htm

Tsuzuki, Chuschichi The Life of Eleanor Marx: A Socialist Tragedy, (Oxford, Clarendon Press, 1967).

Vogel, Lise, Marxism, and the Oppression of Women: Towards a Unitary Theory.    (Illinois, Haymarket Books, 2013).

Williams, Raymond Problems of Materialism (London, Verso 1980).

## Heinrich Heine: poet and revolutionary.

'Ask me not what I have, but what I am.' – Heinrich Heine.

Heinrich Heine was born 1797 in Germany. He was both an important poet in the German 'Romantic' tradition and a revolutionary socialist. These two combines to make Heine pertinent today and a significant figure in proletarian literature. Why? The answer is to be located in the complex interactions between socio-economic forces in the context of History', we may define this as 'Historical Materialism', and the role of the poet in 'alienating' bourgeois conditions i.e. in the relations of Capitalism. Firstly, this analysis will briefly define the methodology described as Historical Materialism which is then applied to the crucial question of the 'alienated 'Romantic poet'. Four main areas of inquiry will be examined in that context: a) biographical details and Heine's textual material b) the place of Heine in the context of the friendship with Marx and Engels, c) the significance of his role as a poet in the revolutionary movement, d) and finally draw the lessons for the oppressed today we can draw from Heine. Therefore, I will illustrate the methodological orientation for this study which is 'Historical Materialism'. Basically there are two essential philosophical categories which have, indeed, sub-sections. They are 'Idealism' and Materialism':

'The great basic question of all philosophy is that concerning the relation of thinking and being...which the philosophers have split into two

great camps...the camp of Idealism and the various schools of Materialism.
- Engels: 'Ludwig Feuerbach.'

I would like to stress here that the terms 'Idealism' and 'Materialism' are here employed in a specific usage is which described by Maurice Cornforth:
'1) Idealism asserts that the material world is dependent on the spiritual. 2) Idealism asserts that that spirit, or mind, or idea, can and do exist in separation from matter. 3) Idealism asserts that there exists a realm of the mysterious and unknowable, 'above', or 'beyond' or 'behind' what can be ascertained and known by perception, experience and science.'
-Maurice Cornforth: 'Materialism and the Dialectical Method''.

This is not just an abstract debate but is one that has a direct consequence on the future of humanity because mistakes in theory lead to errors on practice and if the 'Universal Class', the proletariat and their vanguard party make them the repercussions are immense. If we choose an incorrect methodology, a wrong way of looking and understanding the world we cannot make the correct 'concrete analysis of concrete situations' (Lenin). So, what is 'Materialism': firstly, it is the instrument which the working class and its Party arm themselves in the sense of any closed up, fossilized doctrine...

On the contrary: The whole genus of Marx consists in his giving answers to questions which the progressive thinking of humanity had already posed.'

Lenin: 'The Three Sources and Component Parts of Marxism'. Having established the method used in this paper it is necessary to examine the role of the poet, the estranged poet. Trotsky had commented that poets have to:

'...reshape the world of feelings. Not everybody is capable of that.'

- Trotsky: 'Literature and Revolution'. Heine also commented on the estranged poet in bourgeois society: 'Since the heart of the poet is the central point of the world it must at present times be woefully torn. Those who are able to boost that their hearts have remained whole are only admitting that they have a prosaic narrow heart'. - Heine. Heine was a poet in the tradition of German romanticism which was initially a feudal reaction to the French revolution and the English industrial revolution and it flourished during the reaction of its collapse. But some had supported the French Revolution and were profoundly disappointed by its failure. Hence among this group of poets and intellectuals appeared a revolutionary dimension to German Romanticism that began to rise of which Heine was a part. Therefore, but avoiding idealist analysis, we can understand how poets such as Heine embraced the cause of the oppressed and marginalized. Heine's life and work can be seen clearly in the tradition of a combination of the 'new' with a love of popular culture and folklore. Of course, the 'new' at the time included mould breaking composers such as Ludwig Beethoven who has now been appropriated by elements within the

Establishment. The 'novel' was developing into a revolutionary art form challenging the courtly literature of medieval time. The young Heine was caught up in this cauldron. However, two unrequited loves who haunted him throughout his life, both were cousins: Amalie and Therese. In poems such as: 'allnachtlich im traume' he expresses the intensity of his emotions: raw and spontaneous. Here is the first verse translated into a popular version by the Marxist Hal Draper: 'Nightly I hear you in dreams – you speak With kindness sincerest I throw myself, weeping aloud and weak At your sweet feet, my dearest.' - Heine. Many have known these emotions, indeed some the acts themselves when intoxicated by love. This was published in a collection called: 'Book of Songs' in 1827. Around this time, perhaps heart-broken, and certainly by politically motivation an atmosphere of cynicism combined by a mockery of authority becomes apparent and will continue in much of his work. Six years earlier the 'move' to the political was becoming apparent in his playwriting, in 'Almansor' the servant of the protagonist comments at a public book burning ceremony:

'This was only a prelude; where they burn books they will eventually burn people'. - Heine.

This was certainly a portent of things to come, especially from the pen of a German Jew. Heine's work is rooted in the socio-political, it has its foundation in material reality but clearly transcends the 'mechanistic materialism' which was the 'ideology' of the rising bourgeois, and their world was the triumph of the machine. Engels states without equivocation:

> 'The materialism of the last (18th) century was primary mechanistic.'
>
> - Engels. 'Feuerbach and the rise of 'Classical German Philosophy'.

Heine's work does not exist in a dimension of 'abstractions' (Idealism), it does not tell fairy-stories which are told outside of history. Neither can his writing be understood within a worldview which works like a giant clock sprung into motion by a First Cause and in constant motion until it somehow achieves ultimate perfection, a concept derived originally from Aristotle and integrated into Christian theology by Thomas Aquinas. Equally he goes beyond a world only experienced robotically by sensual experience as described by John Locke. His work is sensual yet transcendent and has the resonance which is, to employ a phrase of the Marxist critic Walter Benjamin, 'free, spontaneous utterance of the creature' as in the poem: Desperately Seeking...

> 'God knows where that crazy woman's Found herself a place to stay;
>
> I've been looking for her in this Cursed rain for half the day'. - Heine.

He required a revolutionary perspective in which to articulate his innovations. He would become aware of this as a consequence of leaving Germany in 1831. Heine moved to France where he would spend the rest of his life. Here he would meet people like the feminist writer and revolutionary George Sand. It was during these early years in Paris that Heine met Karl Marx and mixed with a Utopian socialist group, the Saint-Simonists, these were pivotal moments. Heine would never embrace the fully articulated system created by Marx and Engels; 'Scientific Socialism' but he was writing for the young Marx's weekly journal 'Vorwarts' in the early 1830's. His writing now developed a clear revolutionary socialist tone with poems such as The Weavers Song' which was about an insurrection of weavers in 1844:

'From darkened eyes no tears are falling
With gritted teeth we sit here calling Germany, listen, ere we disperse,
We weave your shroud with a triple curse
We weave we are weaving. - Heine.

This was written in the same year as Marx wrote his great study of 'alienation' and 'struggle': Economic and Philosophical Manuscripts'. Heine also caught the revolutionary consciousness inherent in the proletariat. As with all utopian socialists, which often draw on a 'primitive Christianity' Heine did not understand the inevitable consequence of the rise of capitalism was a working-class revolution which would create more for the majority in a higher synthesis both materially and culturally. Rather he tended to see socialism as a kind of sensual monastic community. Nevertheless, Marx was an admirer of Heinz's work and maintained a close friendship as his daughter Eleanor Marx wrote: 'He loved him just as much as his works, and was as indulgent as can be towards his political weaknesses.

poets, he declared, are peculiar people. You cannot measure them with the usual scale for normal people'.
- Eleanor Marx: Neue Zeit.

Heine's poem 'Germany: A Winter's Tale' provides us with a vision of the future:
'A new song, a better song, oh friends I'll sing for you. here on earth, we mean to make our paradise comes true. we mean to be happy here on earth.
- Heine.
Heinrich Heine was both a great Romantic poet and a revolutionary writer. His flaw was an inability to differentiate the utopian from the authentic revolutionary traditions, a poet of his times and still an inspiration to the oppressed today.

Nigel Pearce

## On the revolutionary poetry of Bertolt Brecht.

'The poet has watched the people's mouth.' - Bertolt Brecht. Bertolt Brecht is probably best known for his experimental plays and the dramatic theory he developed around them. But he was also one of the most important poets of the 20th century and arguably the most significant Marxist poet of this epoch, he wrote 1,500 poems. But he also entered into the debates over the nature of 'Socialist Realism', which he deplored, with Lukacs in the 1920s/30s, a polemic which divided Marxist aesthetics into the 1960's and beyond. Therefore this analysis will address these issues: 1) what were the conditions and circumstances that moulded Brecht's creative work and aesthetics 2) the debate between Brecht and Lukacs on the nature of socialist writing 3) the content and nature of Brecht's Marxist poetry and 4) Brecht's great error of not actively supporting a worker's uprising in East Berlin in 1953 which was crushed by Russian military power and his subsequent withdrawal from the field of Marxist poetry and aesthetics and 6) Brecht's impact on the Situationist International. Brecht was born in 1898 and would therefore experience all the major events which shaped the 20th century until 1956. Of course, the first crisis was the First World War which Lenin had correctly analysed as the result of competing Capitals exporting 'finance capital' in an attempt to stabilize and expand their own capitalist economies and the inevitable conflict which would ensue i.e. World War 1. Brecht was a military orderly towards the end of the war and this experience of imperialist war and its bloody results were an important developmental factor for the young Brecht. No longer would the tradition of Goethe and Romanticism dominate German literature; the world had been objectively changed. An early poem by Brecht captures his horror of and the hypocrisy of the war (Brecht had not had access to Marxist of Leninist writing at this time) called:

> 'The Legend of the Dead soldier'
> 'And when the war was four springs old
> And of peace there was not a breath
> The soldier took the logical step
> And died a hero's death.
> The war however was not yet done
> So the Kaiser was displeased to be sure
> That the soldier had given up like that
> To him it seemed premature.

The soldier is then dug up and pronounced fit for active service. Accompanied by an army Chaplin and draped in a German flag he is escorted through cheering crowds on his way back to the front line. So many were dancing around him now That the soldier could hardly be seen You could only see him from the sky above And there only stars can gleam ... The stars are not forever there. Daylight gives new breath.' - Bertolt Brecht. The next significant stage was Brecht being introduced, by two women who were both committed communists and also lovers of Brecht named Helene Weigel and Elisabeth Hauptmann, too classical Marxist texts. Hauptmann noted in her workbook on 25th October 1926:

> 'Brecht obtains works on socialism and Marxism and

asks for lists of the basic works to study first.'
- Elisabeth Hauptmann.

By 1929 and the Wall Street Crash, which the Great Depression of the 1930s followed, Brecht had studied Marxist economics and philosophy, some Lenin and early Mao Tse-tung on dialectics and the role of the artist in the revolutionary and struggle. But fascism was on the rise throughout Europe; now Brecht was ideologically prepared for it and in this poem delineates what he believed should be the attitude of the poet towards it: 'Within me here is a conflict between delight in the blooming apple-tree And the horror of the painter's* speeches. But only the second Drives me to my desk.' - Bertolt Brecht *Brecht always referred to Hitler as 'the painter' because he had been a house painter. Therefore, it is possible to discern four elements in the formation of Brecht's poetry: 1) imperialist war, 2) embracing Marxism as a worldview, 3) the inevitable decline of capitalism and 4) the rise of fascism. His aesthetic was rooted in the class-struggle; you can perceive his use of everyday language and form. Brecht's position became: 'For art to become "unpolitical" means only to ally itself with the 'ruling group" - Bertolt Brecht. However during this period there was a debate within Marxism regarding the correct 'line' on literature. Lukcas argued, in the 1920/30's, that 19th century realist novels reveal the true horrors of capitalism with 'typical' characters, hence the need for 'socialist realist' novels. Brecht disagreed and argued that the 19th century realist form is outdated and has no capacity to radicalize the oppressed and that new 'dialectical' forms were necessary. He argued in the 1930's against those who pursued the official Moscow 'line' of socialist realism:

'They are, to put it bluntly, enemies of production. Production makes them feel uncomfortable. You never know where you are with production; production is unforeseeable. you never know what's going to come out. And they themselves don't want to produce. They want to play the apparatchik and exercise control over other people.'

## Bertolt Brecht.

Marx and Engels were against 'applied tendency' in literature and Marx described it as: 'The most wretched offal of socialist literature.' - Karl Marx. Brecht used everyday language in his poetry, but he poses a dialectical question, it demands a response. In the poem: 'The Sixteen-Year-Old Seamstress Emma Ries before the Magistrate' Brecht exhibits two essential aspects of his poetry; 1) that it is worker cantered and 2) that it incorporates a knowledge and application of Dialectical Materialism, the science of the proletariat. The poem is about a sixteen-year-old working-class woman who has been caught distributing revolutionary leaflets. She is in a material situation, not in the vacuous spheres of bourgeois speculation. It is also the inevitable dialectical situation workers are objectively drawn into...she conflicts with the oppressors. So here is the dialectical contradiction and how Brecht does resolve this contradiction, of course in the same manner the working class must ultimately resolve it, by revolutionary synthesis: 'As reply, she stood up and sang the Internationale When the magistrate shook his head She shouted: 'Stand up! This is the Internationale!' - Bertolt Brecht. Therefore, it is clear that in his poetry Brecht is creating a new tradition in German poetry, moving away from the themes and methods of Goethe and the Romantics and towards the future of communism. However once ensconced in the German Democratic Republic in the role of Staatsdicher (state poet), a role he was never comfortable in Brecht made the biggest mistake of his life. It was 1953 and a spontaneous worker's uprising erupted in East Berlin, after hesitation he finally supported the Stalinist elite in calling for Russian tanks to crush the revolt. He never recovered from this error and retreated into rustic silence and a poetic wasteland. But Brecht was not entirely curbed by this error and in the aftermath of the rebellion wrote one of his best anti-Stalinist/anti-capitalist poems:

'The Solution.'
Would it not be easier?
In that case for the government
To dissolve the people
And elect another.
- Bertolt Brecht.

Finally I would like to examine the relationship between Brecht and the Situationist International's concept of detournement 'anything can be used' (Guy Debord) to disrupt the alienation within the 'Society of the Spectacle.' To put it more abruptly: 'Plagiarism is necessary. Progress implies it.' (Debord). It is necessary to place this in the context that for the Situationist art was concluded when the Spartacus League failed to bring German dada to fruition in the workers revolution of 1919. They reflected with pleasure that Brecht had commented: 'That he had made some cuts in the classics of theatre in order to make the performances more educative...close to the revolutionary orientation we are calling for.' - Debord/Wolman. Brecht encapsulates his aesthetic in the poem:

'Hymn to Communism'.
'It is so simple which is so difficult.'

## On dialectics and Marxism: a philosophy for today.

'Dialectical materialism is more than a philosophical system it is a philosophy of action.'
- George Plekhanov.

Here is an explanation of the philosophical concepts which inspired and re-enforced much of the confrontation which occurred between rightist members of staff and myself. The theoreticians of the bourgeoisie, in their many manifestations from the academic to that of the padre who condones imperialism, exhibit a single and constant intellectual position in their opposition to the philosophical system of the oppressed which is dialectical materialism. The bourgeoisie are compelled to do so by their objective position in the class system of 'late-capitalism'. They are obliged not only to accumulate Capital but must, therefore, also reproduce the system of ideas. This is because ideas are created by the reproduction of the economic or material life of capitalism. In the same way the proletariat are placed in opposition to capitalism and its dominant ideas because they are economically exploited and also oppressed by bourgeois ideology. The masses are therefore drawn into opposition against capitalism and, ultimately, they are the agents of its overthrow:
'The emancipation of the proletariat is the task of the proletariat.'
- Karl Marx.

Hence the philosophy of the working class can only be forged in the furnace of the class struggle and its theoreticians must move with the motion of historical necessity which is the inevitability of proletarian revolution. So we can see how Marxist philosophy did not materialize in the minds of Marx, Engels, Plekhanov, Lenin and Trotsky spontaneously, but rather it was the consequence of the proletariat and its intellectuals learning the lessons of the class struggle.

Leon Trotsky (1879-1940), one of a vanguard of Marxist thinkers, maintained that in the process of the development of human ideas:

'Two systems of logic are worthy of attention; the logic of Aristotle (formal logic) and the logic of Hegel (dialectical logic).
- Leon Trotsky.

More than 2,000 years ago Greek philosophers who were exploring the human mind and the natural world discovered the dialectic:

'The ancient Greeks were all natural-born dialecticians and had already analyses the most essential forms of dialectical thought'.
- Fredrick Engels.
This is clearly illustrated in the work of Heraclitus (540-480BC) who argued that:
'Everything is and is not, for everything

is fluid, is constantly changing, constantly coming into being and passing away'.
- Heraclitus..

We can locate the essence of dialectics, which is impermanence, here in the thought of Heraclitus. The concept of 'logic' which is derived from the Greek 'logos' meaning 'word' or 'reason' formed the basis on which Aristotle (384-322 BC) constructed the model of formal logic. This became the dominant form for much human intellectual endeavour. He discerned three main laws in formal logic:

1) The Law of identity: A=A.

2) The Law of contradiction: A cannot be A and non-A.

3) The Law of the excluded middle: A is either A or non-A.

## Aristotle

These three principles of logic are the foundation of modern science and mathematics. Aristotle's model of logic dominated Western thought intermittently for about 2, 000 years and appears to be 'common sense'. But 'common sense' does not look below the surface appearance of nature and the processes of History. We can begin to perceive the limitations of formal logic and to become aware of the scope of dialectical logic. As Trotsky commented:
'Dialectical understanding is not limited to the problems of daily life, but attempts to arrive at an understanding of a more complicated and drawn-our process. Dialectical and formal logic bear a relationship similar to that between higher and lower mathematics'.
- Leon Trotsky..

The limitations of formal logic or what Trotsky sometimes called 'vulgar thought' became clear with the rise of modern science. An enormous blow to the bourgeoisie and their lackeys was Charles Darwin's theory of evolution. This theory proved that one species can be transformed into another and that therefore qualitative change outside the static categories of formal logic takes place. Trotsky commented:

The fundamental flaw in vulgar thought lies in the fact that it wishes to content itself with motionless imprints of reality which consists of eternal motion.'
- Leon Trotsky..

Therefore modern science needed a philosophical system to create a theoretical model to explain its discoveries, this theory is dialectical materialism. The roots of modern dialectics lie in radical German philosophy which had been inspired by the French revolution of 1789 and the collapse of the old order. The major thinker of this progressive wave was George F. Hegel G (1770-1831). He studied the Greek dialecticians and combined their insight about the transitory and interconnected nature of reality with German naturphilosophie or 'Philophy of Nature'. His orientation was essentially one of metaphysics i.e. he saw reality as 'ideas' or 'spirit' rather than 'matter in motion'. However Hegel's philosophy of dialectics challenged the mechanistic ideas about motion which had become dominant. For Hegel there were three stages in the dialectical process:

1) Simple unity, the object before any change.
2) The negation, this is when the object creates its opposite.
3) The negation of the negation when the opposites are reconciled in a higher synthesis.

Hegel believed everything existed in the mind of God. His whole system was to show how these three moments of the dialectic, described above, are acted out by the 'Absolute Spirit' or 'Absolute Idea', which are ultimately terms for God, in History. The three stages described above became:
1) The simple unity of God.
2) God creating his negation which is Nature.

3) The unification of God and Nature through the development of human
consciousness into a higher union.
To understand this it is necessary to see it in the context of Hegel's ideas about the progress of human consciousness:
1) The simple unity of the isolated human mind.
2) The separation of the human mind from nature which Hegel called alienation.
3) Unification of the human mind with nature in the higher synthesis with the
'Absolute Spirit' or God.

Interestingly Hegel believed that this higher synthesis of the human mind, Nature and the 'Absolute Spirit' was made possible by his philosophical system. So, we can see how Hegel, as a result of the rise of radical German philosophy which was influenced by revolutionary France, created a system of ideas which transcended the limitations of formal logic and 'vulgar thought', but:

'Hegel fell into the illusion of conceiving the real as the product of thought, the real subject retains its autonomous existence outside the head'.
- Karl Marx.

This means that for Marx (1818-1883) reality did not reside in thought or spirit but in the world, we see around us i.e. 'outside the head'. Hegel had advanced the concept of the dialectic; however, it was with Marx's critique of Hegel that a major leap in philosophy took place. Marx said:

'The dialectic is standing on its head. It
must be inverted in order to discover the
rational kernel within the mystical shell'.
- Karl Marx.

It was with this analysis that Marx created the
flowering of ideas which is dialectical materialism.
This is the philosophy that every class-conscious
worker needs in his or her daily battle with
bourgeois ideology and is the system of ideas that
prepares the path for worker's revolution.
Three basic laws are at the core of dialectical
materialism and as a whole they form a coherent
system. They comprise of:

'The general laws of motion and
development of nature, human
society and though.'
    - Fredrick Engels.

The Law of the Unity and Struggle of Opposites.
Lenin (1870-1924) summed this up:
'The condition for the knowledge
of all processes of life of the world
…in their real life is the knowledge
of them as a unity of opposites.'
- V. I. Lenin.

Let us consider two consequences of this:

a) 'non-being' must contain its opposite 'being'
within itself, in the same way 'being' must contain
'non-being'. Therefore, the bourgeois argument for
the necessity of a 'First Cause' to set the
clockwork of the universe in motion is

unnecessary because 'non-being' or 'nothing' created its opposite 'being' or 'existence' at the beginning of Time.

b) In capitalism the bourgeois and the proletariat are bound together by the system, yet they also exist as material and antagonistic opposites which creates the class struggle.

2) The Law of the Transformation of Quantity into Quality.

Engels (1820-1895) defines this law:

'We could express this by saying that in nature...qualitative changes can only happen with the quantitative addition or subtraction of motion'.

- Fredrick Engels.

An example of this would be that when heat is applied to water and the temperature of the water changes a quantitative change takes place, but when the water becomes steam a qualitative transformation has taken place. Similarly we can see how a series of quantitative changes takes place in a capitalist society e.g. trade union struggles and how these inevitably lead to a 'dialectical leap' or qualitative change i.e. proletarian revolution. Learning from the lessons of History Lenin developed this position:

'Capitalism creates its own gravedigger, itself creates the elements for a new system...without a 'leap' these individual elements change nothing'.
- V.I. Lenin.

Hence Lenin ascertained that there is no reformist path to socialism, there must be a 'leap', a revolution.

3) The Law of the Negation of the Negation.

In capitalism a process called the 'negation of the negation' takes place. This essentially means that the 'thesis' or first aspect of a dialectical contradiction is not destroyed by its opposite or 'antithesis' and some aspects of both the 'thesis' and the 'antitheses survive within a higher 'synthesis'. The 'negation' is in the class conflict between workers and bosses which creates the 'negation of the negation' that is proletarian revolution and socialism. The result of the 'negation of the negation' is a classless society, a society without contradictions. Marx examined the concept in Capital:

'The capitalist mode of appropriation is the first negation of individual private property based on one's labour. But capitalist production begets with the inevitability of a natural process its own negation. It is the negation of the negation.'
- Karl Marx.

What tactics should revolutionaries pursue? Ulrike Meinhoff (1934-1975) argued in 1971:
'That a pre-requisite for progress and an eventual victory of revolutionary forces is the armed struggle.'
- Ulrike Meinhoff.

But today the conditions of the class struggle have changed, and we must again win the battle of ideas, an ideological hegemony, to prepare for the inevitable revolution. Today:

'Dialectics are our sharpest weapons'.
- Fredrick Engels.

www.ingramcontent.com/pod-product-compliance
Ingram Content Group UK Ltd.
Pitfield, Milton Keynes, MK11 3LW, UK
UKHW041410180426
11947UKWH00007B/48